Children with Mental Disorder and the Law

of related interest

Young Children's Rights
Exploring Beliefs, Principles and Practice
2nd edition
Priscilla Alderson
Forewords by Save the Children and Mary John
ISBN 978 1 84310 599 2
Children in Charge series

Disabled Children and the Law
Research and Good Practice
2nd edition
Janet Read, Luke Clements and David Ruebain
ISBN 978 1 84310 280 9

Community Care Practice and the Law
3rd edition
Michael Mandelstam
ISBN 978 1 84310 233 5

See You in Court
A Social Worker's Guide to Presenting Evidence in Care Proceedings
Lynn Davis
ISBN 978 1 84310 547 3

Morals, Rights and Practice in the Human Services
Effective and Fair Decision-Making in Health, Social Care and Criminal Justice
Marie Connolly and Tony Ward
ISBN 978 1 84310 486 5

The Nearest Relative Handbook
David Hewitt
ISBN 978 1 84310 522 0

Developing Advocacy for Children and Young People
Current Issues in Research, Policy and Practice
Edited by Christine M. Oliver and Jane Dalrymple
Foreword by Cherie Booth QC
ISBN 978 1 84310 596 1

Children
with Mental
Disorder
and the Law
A Guide to Law and Practice

Anthony Harbour

Jessica Kingsley Publishers
London and Philadelphia

First published in 2008
by Jessica Kingsley Publishers
116 Pentonville Road
London N1 9JB, UK
and
400 Market Street, Suite 400
Philadelphia, PA 19106, USA

www.jkp.com

Copyright © Anthony Harbour 2008
Chapters 9 and 10 copyright © Jessica Kingsley Publishers 2008

Library of Congress Cataloging in Publication Data
A CIP catalog record for this book is available from the Library of Congress

British Library Cataloguing in Publication Data
A CIP catalogue record for this book is available from the British Library

ISBN 978 1 84310 576 3

Printed and bound in Great Britain by
Athenaeum Press, Gateshead, Tyne and Wear

Contents

Part 1 The Law

Introduction 19; The United Nations Convention on the Rights of the Child (UNCRC) 19; Human Rights Act 1998 (HRA) 22; Conclusions 32; Case examples 33

Introduction 34; 1 – Parental responsibility 35; 2 – Children Act principles 37; 3 – Private law proceedings 40; 4 – Public law proceedings 41; Conclusions 47; Case examples 48

Introduction 49; Restriction of liberty without court order 50; Court proceedings 51; Family proceedings 51; Criminal proceedings 51; Definition of secure accommodation 52; Who can apply for a secure accommodation order? 53; The duty to avoid placing children in secure accommodation 54; The length of the order 54; Minimum age 55; Interrelationship between the MHA and section 25 55; The accommodated child 55; The application of the welfare principle in court proceedings 56; Control and restraint of children 56; Conclusions 58; Case example 58

Part 2 Practice Issues

Part 3 Problem Areas

Preface

In 1999 the Richardson Committee (the committee that was established by the government to review the Mental Health Act 1983) wrote:

> ...the law relating to the treatment of children suffering from mental disorder is in need of clarification. The current multiplicity of legal provisions creates a climate of uncertainty, professionals are unsure of their authority and of the legal and ethical entitlements of the children in their care.[1]

Since that date there has been little clarification, and the climate of uncertainty remains. This book simply draws together some of the many 'legal provisions' to assist, in particular mental health professionals, in making sense of the law in this area. It is not a legal textbook, rather a book aimed at practitioners who need to ensure that their practice is both lawful and conforms to 'good practice'.

The book falls into three parts. The first part describes various areas of the law. The second part, comprising two chapters written respectively by an approved social worker (ASW) and a child psychiatrist, focuses on practice issues. The third part covers, more discursively than the previous chapters, particular areas that can cause difficulty in practice.

The book is based on the author's experience of providing training to ASWs and child psychiatrists. The training needs of these two professional groups are separate but interlinked. The ASWs have extensive knowledge of mental health law but are not in the main child care specialists. The child psychiatrists will be by definition specialist in the care and treatment of children and young people but may not have a great deal of experience in

---

1   Department of Health (1999) *Review of the Mental Health Act 1983: Report of the Expert Committee.* London: Department of Health (DH), paragraph 13.1.

using the Mental Health Act 1983. One of the aims of the book is to provide sufficient information to allow each group to understand better the role and responsibilities of their professional colleagues.

The material is based on this training and many of the examples have been developed from discussions that have taken place during this training. The focus on the Mental Health Act 1983 and the Mental Health Act 2007 throughout the text reflects the fact that this book will be used for the continuing training of child psychiatrists and ASWs. (The ASWs will become approved mental health professionals (AMHPs) in October 2008.) The text contains a number of case examples which are inserted for teaching purposes to trigger questions and discussion around some of the problem areas identified in the text.

The law constantly changes and books about the law have to keep up with these changes. During the course of the publication of this book the Mental Health Act 2007 became law. This statute is incorporated in the text even though the Act will in the main become operational in October 2008 at the earliest. In October 2007 the Department of Health published a *Draft revised Code of Practice*. This draft is the subject of consultation and so some parts of the Code are likely to have been changed by the time this book is published.[2]

A particular problem in writing a book about children and the law is the best way to describe the child. The simplest solution is to adopt the definition of a child contained in the Children Act 1989 (CA), that is 'any person under the age of 18'.[3] The problem with this approach is that young people are then referred to as children in contexts that sometimes appear inappropriate. This book therefore moves between using the terms 'child', 'young person' and 'child and young person' as the sense of the text requires. So for example a young person over 16 who falls within the provisions of the Mental Capacity Act 2005 (MCA) is referred to as a 'young person', and a 12-year-old child is referred to as a 'child'.

Another problem with terminology is to describe with consistency the bewildering variety of organisations that a child with mental health difficulties will have to deal with. The following terms are used:

---

2   Department of Health (1999) *Mental Health Act 1983 Code of Practice*. London: DH, and Department of Health (2007) *Mental Health Act 1983 Draft revised Code of Practice*. London: DH. In the text the Codes are referred to as the 1999 Code or the 2007 Draft Code respectively.

3   Children Act 1989, section 105(1).

Child and adolescent mental health services (CAMHS)	A collective description of the organisations responsible for child and adolescent mental health services.
Health authority	A generic description of the organisations that have statutory responsibility for the delivery of health care, both in hospital and the community.
Primary care trusts (PCTs)	The organisations responsible for the delivery of primary health care and also for commissioning community health services including CAMHS.
Mental health trusts and foundation trusts	The organisations responsible for the delivery of specialist mental health services, both in-patient and out-patient, to persons with mental health problems.
Local authority	A generic description of the organisations responsible for the funding and delivery of services at a local level.
Social service authority	A generic description of the organisations that have statutory responsibility for the funding and delivery of local authority children's services.
Children's services	The Children Act 2004 has effectively merged the social service and education responsibilities of local authorities into children's services departments.

A book as derivative as this relies heavily on published material. In particular this book contains some material in a book published in 2004 and co-authored by Richard White, Anthony Harbour and Richard Williams;[4] a particular acknowledgement is therefore made to Richard White and Richard Williams. Some other books that have assisted the authors are listed in Appendix 1: Further Reading.

---

4   White, R., Harbour, A. and Williams, R. (eds) (2004) *Safeguards for Young Minds*, 2nd edn. London: Gaskell.

Note on terminology

This book contains references to a mass of legal material including statutes
(the Children Act 1989), statutory instruments (Children (Secure Accommodation) Regulations 1991) and government guidance (The Mental Health
Act 1983 Code of Practice). The text contains references to particular cases
(Re K (Secure Accommodation Order: Right to Liberty) [2001] 1 FLR 526).
Reported cases are contained in a number of different law reports. The text
refers to various series of law reports which are abbreviated as follows:

FLR   Family Law Reports

All ER   All England Law Reports

EHRR   European Human Rights Reports

MHLR   Mental Health Law Reports

The abbreviation EWHC refers to a unique number furnished to every High
Court judgment from a register kept at the High Court from 2002 onwards.
When the cases are discussed sometimes the text refers to 'the court' as the
decision maker, at other times to the particular judge, for example Mr Justice
Bennett (Bennett J) or Lord Justice Thorpe (Thorpe LJ).

Acknowledgements

I have received enormous assistance in writing this book. In particular I would like to thank: Sue Bailey, Rob Brown, Luke Clements, Anselm Eldergill, Simon Foster, John Horne, Helen Kingston, Penny Letts, Mary Mitchell, Nicola Moxham, Camilla Parker, Kathryn Pugh, Yashi Shah and Wendy Whitaker.

The length of this list does not detract from the fact that all the errors in the text are my own.

Contributors

Mary Mitchell is a consultant child psychiatrist at Leigh House Adolescent Hospital, a specialist in-patient facility for young people managed by Hampshire Partnership NHS Trust, UK. She is involved in the development of child and adolescent mental health services, and trains health professionals, medical students and social workers.

Wendy Whitaker has worked in child protection and mental health for 20 years. She has practised in an inner London community mental health team, the Bethlem and Maudsley in-patient services and an A&E self-harm service. In February 1999 she joined the Gerald Russell Eating Disorders Unit of the South London and Maudsley NHS Trust, working with people aged 14 and upwards. She is now a senior practitioner, and her work includes Mental Health Act work for all the specialist wards, coordinating family work, running a carers' support group and motivational enhancement therapy, as well as providing training in all of these areas.

Part 1
The Law

Chapter 1

Human Rights

Introduction

This chapter deals with the United Nations Convention on the Rights of the Child (UNCRC) and the Human Rights Act 1998 (HRA). The UNCRC was ratified by the UK in 1991. There is no method to directly enforce the UNCRC in the UK courts. By contrast the Human Rights Act 1998 is 'a legally enforceable charter of human rights and fundamental freedoms'.[1] Whilst the UNCRC is specifically focused on the rights of the child the European Convention on Human Rights (ECHR) applies to all persons including children.

The United Nations Convention on the Rights of the Child (UNCRC)

What is the UNCRC?

The following information is from the UNICEF website:

> The Convention on the Rights of the Child is the first legally binding international instrument to incorporate the full range of human rights – civil, cultural, economic, political and social rights. In 1989, world leaders decided that children needed a special convention just for them because people under 18 years old often need special care and protection that adults do not. The leaders also wanted to make sure that the world recognised that children have human rights too.

---

1   Lester, A. and Pannick, D. (2004) *Human Rights Law and Practice*, 2nd edn. London: LexisNexis.

The Convention sets out these rights in 54 articles and two Optional Protocols. It spells out the basic human rights that children everywhere have: the right to survival; to develop to the fullest; to protection from harmful influences, abuse and exploitation; and to participate fully in family, cultural and social life. The four core principles of the Convention are non-discrimination; devotion to the best interests of the child; the right to life, survival and development; and respect for the views of the child. Every right spelled out in the Convention is inherent to the human dignity and harmonious development of every child. The Convention protects children's rights by setting standards in health care; education; and legal, civil and social services.

By agreeing to undertake the obligations of the Convention (by ratifying or acceding to it), national governments have committed themselves to protecting and ensuring children's rights and they have agreed to hold themselves accountable for this commitment before the international community. States parties to the Convention are obliged to develop and undertake all actions and policies in the light of the best interests of the child.[2]

UNCRC articles

Whilst the UNCRC articles are not directly enforceable in the UK courts they have direct relevance to many of the day-to-day problems faced by children and young people in contact with CAMHS. For example:

ARTICLE 12

The right to express views freely in all matters affecting the child, in particular in judicial and administrative proceedings.

The UNCRC has been considered in a number of English cases. In the case of *Mabon*[3] the court decided that the decision of a judge to refuse to allow three boys aged 17, 15 and 13 to be separately represented in proceedings concerning their choice of residence with their separated parents was incorrect. In arriving at that decision Thorpe LJ referred to the obligations imposed on the state to comply with Article 12 of the UNCRC.

---

2   www.unicef.org/crc (accessed 07.12.07).
3   *Mabon* v. *Mabon* [2005] 2 FLR 1011, page 26.

The article will also have application to 'administrative proceedings' and would therefore include the entitlement of a child to advocacy at, for example, a significant care-planning meeting held within an in-patient unit.

ARTICLE 23

A mentally or physically disabled child should enjoy a full and decent life, in conditions which ensure dignity, promote self-reliance and facilitate the child's active participation in the community.

This article would support a young person's entitlement to adequate after-care services, in particular accommodation following discharge from hospital.

ARTICLE 25

The right of a child who has been placed by the competent authorities for the purpose of care, protection or treatment of his or her physical or mental health, to a periodic review of the treatment provided to the child and all other circumstances relevant to his placement.

The Mental Health Act 1983 provides for the review of a young person's detention. This article goes further and would cover, for example, the review of the in-patient treatment regime of an informal child patient. This, alongside Article 12, would justify review (and representation) at meetings considering the appropriateness of the child's placement as well as the progress of treatment or care.

ARTICLE 37

Every child deprived of liberty shall be separated from adults unless it is considered in the child's interests not to do so.

The government took this article into account in deciding to amend the Mental Health Act 2007[4] to require that the provision of age-appropriate

---

4   Mental Health Act 2007, section 31, amending Mental Health Act 1983, sections 39 and 131.

accommodation for detained children should be taken into account prior to the admission of a child to hospital.[5]

Compliance

By ratification the UK government has committed itself to an external evaluation of compliance by the UN Committee of the Rights of the Child. Periodically the government is expected to send to the Committee a report detailing its compliance with the UNCRC. This report is subject to scrutiny and comment by non-government organisations. A final report is then published. Again from the UNICEF website:

> Governments that ratify the Convention or one of its Optional Protocols must report to the Committee on the Rights of the Child, the body of experts charged with monitoring States' implementation of the Convention and Optional Protocols. These reports outline the situation of children in the country and explain the measures taken by the State to realise their rights. In its reviews of States' reports, the Committee urges all levels of government to use the Convention as a guide in policy-making and implementation. And because the protection of human rights is by nature a permanent and endless process, there is always room for improvement.

Human Rights Act 1998 (HRA)

The Human Rights Act 1998 became operational in October 2000. Its key provisions are as follows.

SECTION 2

This section requires UK courts and tribunals to take account of the judgements, decisions, declarations or opinions of the institutions established by the Convention when determining a question which has arisen in connection with a Convention right.

---

5   Mental Health Act 2007 and *Pushed into the Shadows: Young People's Experience of Adult Mental Health Facilities*. London: Office of the Children's Commissioner, January 2007.

SECTION 3

This section requires primary and subordinate legislation to be interpreted and applied consistently with Convention rights, so far as possible.

The application of section 3 can be illustrated by the case of *E* v. *Bristol City Council.*[6] In that case the court was considering the requirement, contained in the Mental Health Act 1983, to consult a nearest relative 'where reasonably practicable'. Bennett J interpreted section 11 of the Mental Health Act in a way which was compatible with the patient's rights under Article 8; in that way her wish not to have her relative consulted was achieved.

SECTION 4

This section sets out the circumstances in which the courts may make a declaration of incompatibility.

Under section 4 a declaration of incompatibility may be made by certain courts, that is the High Court, the Court of Appeal and the House of Lords. This allows those courts to make a declaration when they are satisfied that the provisions of a particular statute are incompatible with ECHR rights. In the case of *H,*[7] the court held that the provisions of the Mental Health Act 1983, which placed the burden upon the patient to prove that the criteria justifying his detention in hospital for treatment no longer exist, was incompatible with the ECHR (Article 5). The government therefore amended the Mental Health Act.

SECTION 6

This section imposes a duty on public authorities to act in a manner compatible with Convention rights. An exception to this duty[8] is where a public authority is required by primary legislation to take the action in question. Public authority includes any person for whom certain functions are of a public nature.[9]

---

6   *E* v. *Bristol City Council* [2005] EWHC 74 (Admin) CO/4464/2004.

7   *R (H)* v. *London North and East Region Mental Health Review Tribunal (Secretary of State intervening)* [2001] EWCA Civ 415.

8   Human Rights Act 1998, section 6(2)(a).

9   Ibid., section 6(3).

Public authority is not defined in the Act. However, health and local authorities are clearly public authorities, therefore health and social care professionals working for CAMHS are subject to the section 6 duty. Professionals working for private health and social care providers are also subject to this provision if the functions they perform are of a 'public nature'.[10] A consultant psychiatrist working in a private hospital with responsibility for the treatment of a young person detained under the Mental Health Act 1983 is performing a function which is of a public nature.[11] Generally doctors are public authorities in relation to their NHS functions, but not in relation to their private patients.

Rights Protected under the Human Rights Act 1998

- The right to life (Article 2).

- Protection from torture and inhuman or degrading treatment or punishment (Article 3).

- Protection from slavery and forced or compulsory labour (Article 4).

- The right to liberty and security of person (Article 5).

- The right to fair trial (Article 6).

- Protection from retrospective criminal offences (Article 7).

- The protection of private and family life (Article 8).

- Freedom of thought and conscience and religion (Article 9).

- Freedom of association and assembly (Article 11).

- The right to marry and found a family (Article 12).

- Freedom from discrimination in relation to Convention rights (Article 14).

---

10 The House of Lords decided that a private care home providing care and accommodation for elderly people did not fall within section 6(3) of the Human Rights Act 1998 (HRA). *YL* v *Birmingham City Council and others* [2007] 3 All ER 957–1006.

11 *R (A)* v. *Partnerships in Care Ltd* [2002] EWHC 529.

Principles of interpretation

Complicated rules and procedures have developed in this area of law. For example:

1. *The ECHR as living instrument*
    The ECHR 'is a living instrument which...must be interpreted in the light of present-day conditions'.[12] The case of *Nielsen* v. *Denmark*[13] (discussed below) provides an illustration of how this principle might be applied.

2. *Margin of appreciation*
    This refers to the latitude allowed to member states in their observation of the Convention.[14]

3. *The principle of proportionality*
    A restriction on a freedom guaranteed by the Convention must be 'proportionate to the legitimate aim pursued'.[15] This requires the need to find a fair balance between the protection of individual rights and the interests of the whole community.

4. *Positive obligations*
    Some of the key ECHR articles are couched in the negative, for example in Article 5 the state is required not to unlawfully imprison people. European Convention case law recognises that in some circumstances the state may have positive obligations. In *A* v. *United Kingdom*[16] the European Court held that states are required to take measures to ensure that individuals within their jurisdiction are not subjected to inhuman or degrading treatment or punishment, in this case corporal punishment carried out by A's stepfather.

Convention rights considered

The following articles have particular significance in relation to the management and treatment of children and young people with mental health difficulties.

---

12   *Tyrer* v. *United Kingdom* (1978) 2 EHRR 1, page 10.
13   *Nielsen* v. *Denmark* (1989) 11 EHRR 175.
14   *Handyside* v. *UK* (1976) 1 EHRR 737.
15   *Handyside* v. *UK* (1976), page 754.
16   *A* v. *United Kingdom* (1998) 27 EHRR 611.

ARTICLE 3

No one shall be subjected to torture or to inhuman or degrading treatment or punishment.

This article could apply when the provision of psychiatric treatment to a child is being considered. The courts have set a high threshold in relation to the application of the article.[17] This would not preclude challenge to the provision of psychiatric treatment of a child where the evidence base for the treatment was uncertain, for example the use of ECT.

ARTICLE 5

1. Everyone has the right to liberty and security of person. No one shall be deprived of his liberty save in the following cases and in accordance with a procedure prescribed by law:

   a. the lawful detention of a person after conviction by a competent court;

   b. the lawful arrest or detention of a person for non-compliance with the lawful order of a court or in order to secure the fulfilment of any obligation prescribed by law;

   c. the lawful arrest or detention of a person effected for the purpose of bringing him before the competent legal authority on reasonable suspicion of having committed an offence or when it is reasonably considered necessary to prevent his committing an offence or fleeing after having done so;

   d. the detention of a minor by lawful order for the purpose of educational supervision or his lawful detention for the purpose of bringing him before the competent legal authority;

---

17   *Herczegalvy* v. *Austria* (1993) 15 EHRR 437. In the domestic courts there have been a number of cases under the Human Rights Act concerning the provision of treatment to adult psychiatric patients. These include: *R (Wilkinson)* v. (1) *Broadmoor Hospital Authority,* (2) *the Mental Health Act Commission,* (3) *Secretary of State for Health* (2002) 1 WLR 419; *R (N)* v. *Dr M and others* (2002) EWCA Civ 1789; *R (PS)* v. *RMO and SOAD* (2003) EWHC 2335; *R (B)* v. *Dr SS and others* (2005) EWCA Civ 28; and *R (JB)* v. *Haddock and others* (2006) EWCA Civ 961.

e. the lawful detention of persons for the prevention of the spreading of infectious diseases, of persons of unsound mind, alcoholics or drug addicts or vagrants;

f. the lawful arrest or detention of a person to prevent his effecting an unauthorised entry into the country or of a person against whom action is being taken with a view to deportation or extradition.

2. Everyone who is arrested shall be informed promptly, in a language which he understands, of the reasons for his arrest and of any charge against him.

3. Everyone arrested or detained in accordance with the provisions of paragraph 1.c. of this article shall be brought promptly before a judge or other officer authorised by law to exercise judicial power and shall be entitled to trial within a reasonable time or to release pending trial. Release may be conditioned by guarantees to appear for trial.

4. Everyone who is deprived of his liberty by arrest or detention shall be entitled to take proceedings by which the lawfulness of his detention shall be decided speedily by a court and his release ordered if the detention is not lawful.

5. Everyone who has been the victim of arrest or detention in contravention of the provisions of this article shall have an enforceable right to compensation.

Meaning of 'deprivation of liberty'

Both the European Court of Human Rights (ECtHR) and domestic courts have considered, in relation to adults, the notion of deprivation of liberty contained in Article 5(1).

In the case of *Guzzardi* the European Court said that:

In order to determine whether some one has been 'deprived of his liberty' within the meaning of Article 5, the starting point must be his concrete situation and account must be taken of a whole range of criteria such as the type, duration, effects and manner of implementation of the measure in question.[18]

In the case of *HL* v. *UK*[19] the European Court decided that treating an incapacitated adult for some three months in a psychiatric hospital outside a statutory framework offering protection, in this case the Mental Health Act 1983, whilst he was deprived of liberty, violated the patient's Article 5 rights.

The impact of these cases is that public authorities appear to have adopted a more considered approach to circumstances where an individual may be deprived of their liberty. The government has also responded to the *HL* judgment by introducing statutory safeguards for incapacitated adults.[20]

Although domestic law provides statutory safeguards for children or young people where there is a deprivation of liberty, which are compatible with Article 5, there remains some uncertainty as to whether the authorisation of treatment by a parent requires different considerations to be applied.

In the case of *Nielsen* v. *Denmark*[21] the court considered the case of a 12-year-old boy, Jon Nielsen, who had been admitted to a child psychiatric ward. The duration of his treatment as an in-patient was five-and-a-half months, with the restrictions imposed on him being gradually relaxed as his treatment progressed. The court analysed the extent to which Jon's actual situation amounted to a deprivation of liberty within Article 5. It took into account a number of factors (for example, he was allowed to leave the ward with permission) in deciding that there had been no such deprivation. The court concluded that any restrictions on his movement did not amount to a

---

18   *Guzzardi* v. *Italy* (1980) 3 EHRR 333.
19   *HL* v. *UK* Application No. 45508/99 [2005].
       Also see the case of *DE*: 'I agree, therefore, with Mr Bowen and Ms Richards when they identify the crucial issue here as being, just as it was in *HL* v. *United Kingdom* (2004) 40 EHRR 761, whether DE was or was not, is or is not, "free to leave". And I agree with them when they submit that DE was not and is not "free to leave", and was and is, in that sense, completely under the control of SCC, because, as Ms Richards put it, it was and is SCC who decides the essential matters of where DE can live, whether he can leave and whether he can be with JE.' Paragraph 117 in *JE* v. (1) *DE*, (2) *Surrey CC* and (3) *EW* [2006] EWHC 3459 (Fam).
20   Mental Health Act 2007, schedules 7 and 8, amending the Mental Capacity Act 2005.
21   *Nielsen* v. *Denmark* (1988) 11 EHRR 175.

deprivation of liberty and were the consequence of 'a responsible exercise by his mother of her custodial rights in the interests of the child'.[22]

The *Nielsen* case has been criticised. The court's approach was, however, unsurprising. The objective factors that could amount to a deprivation of liberty were evaluated as required in *Guzzardi*. Although it was concluded that there had been no deprivation of liberty in Jon's case the court also accepted that 'the rights of the holder of parental authority cannot be unlimited and that it is incumbent on the State to provide safeguards against abuse'.[23]

By applying the 'living instrument principle' it can be argued that a case involving a child being treated on the basis of parental consent (particularly where deprivation of liberty was the disputed issue) would be approached differently today. This would be for a number of reasons including the following: Jon's wishes and feelings and his competence were never closely analysed; and social attitudes towards both the limits of parental responsibility and the rights of children have changed over the last 20 years with (in particular) the benefits of statutory protection now more clearly recognised.

The limits of parental responsibility were also considered in the case of K.[24] (This was the first case brought under the Human Rights Act in relation to the application of Article 5 to the secure accommodation regime.) K was subject to a secure accommodation order under the Children Act 1989 and one issue to be determined by the court was whether such an order fell within the definition of educational supervision (see below). In deciding this the court considered what actions could fall outside normal standards of acceptable control. Dame Elizabeth Butler-Sloss observed, following an analysis of the *Nielsen* case and recognising the principles set out in the case, that 'there is a point, however, at which one has to stand back and say – is this within ordinary acceptable parental restrictions upon the movements of a child or does it require justification?'[25]

This approach underpins some of the guidance contained in the 2007 Mental Health Act Code of Practice where the term 'the parental zone of responsibility' is introduced.[26]

---

22   *Nielsen* v. *Denmark* (1988) 11 EHRR 175, paragraph 73.
23   *Nielsen* v. *Denmark* (1988) 11 EHRR 175, paragraph 72.
24   *Re K (Secure Accommodation Order: Right to Liberty)* [2001] 1 FLR 526.
25   *Re K*, paragraph 28, page 536.
26   Department of Health (2007) *Mental Health Act 1983 Draft revised Code of Practice.* London: DH, paragraphs 39.42–39.45.

ARTICLE 5(1)(D) – EDUCATIONAL SUPERVISION

Article 5(1)(d) authorises the detention of a minor (this includes the Children Act definition[27] of a child) for the purposes of educational supervision. Following the implementation of the Human Rights Act 1998, the issue of whether a secure accommodation order made under section 25 of the Children Act 1989 fell within Article 5(1)(d) was challenged; the court decided K's detention was lawful and that 'The concept of "educational supervision" goes well beyond either normal parental control or academic lessons taught in the classroom.'[28]

ARTICLE 6

1. In the determination of his civil rights and obligations or of any criminal charge against him, everyone is entitled to a fair and public hearing within a reasonable time by an independent and impartial tribunal established by law. Judgment shall be pronounced publicly but the press and public may be excluded from all or part of the trial in the interests of morals, public order or national security in a democratic society, where the interests of juveniles or the protection of the private life of the parties so require, or to the extent strictly necessary in the opinion of the court in special circumstances where publicity would prejudice the interests of justice.

2. Everyone charged with a criminal offence shall be presumed innocent until proved guilty according to law.

3. Everyone charged with a criminal offence has the following minimum rights:

    a. to be informed promptly, in a language which he understands and in detail, of the nature and cause of the accusation against him;

    b. to have adequate time and facilities for the preparation of his defence;

    c. to defend himself in person or through legal assistance of his own choosing or, if he has not sufficient means to

---

27   Children Act 1989, section 105(1).
28   Re K [2001] 1 FLR 526, page 559, paragraph 116.

> pay for legal assistance, to be given it free when the interests of justice so require;
>
> d. to examine or have examined witnesses against him and to obtain the attendance and examination of witnesses on his behalf under the same conditions as witnesses against him;
>
> e. to have the free assistance of an interpreter if he cannot understand or speak the language used in court.

In the case of *T and V*[29] the European Court held that there had been violations of Article 6 because the ten-year-old defendants (charged and convicted of murder) had not been able to participate effectively in the criminal trial process.

ARTICLE 8

> 1. Everyone has the right to respect for his private and family life, his home and his correspondence.
>
> 2. There shall be no interference by a public authority with the exercise of this right except such as is in accordance with the law and is necessary in a democratic society in the interests of national security, public safety or the economic well-being of the country, for the prevention of disorder or crime, for the protection of health or morals, or for the protection of the rights and freedoms of others.

Article 8 is broad in scope. By way of example it covers both the rights of the parent to make treatment decisions for their children[30] and also the child's right and entitlement to confidentiality about aspects of their medical treatment. Even if an action appears to constitute an interference with Article 8, it may be justified, as wide grounds exist for justifying any interference. Justification on the grounds of the protection of health alone (see the wording of Article 8(2)) usually involves the taking of children into care by public

---

29   *T and V* v. *United Kingdom* [2000] 7 BHRC 659.

30   'It is therefore the case that a violation of this Article [Article 8] is likely to occur if an application is made to detain a child under the Mental Health Act in circumstances where the parents of the child have not been offered the opportunity of being involved in the decision making process.' Jones, R. (2006) *Mental Health Act Manual*, 10th edn. London: Thomson Sweet & Maxwell, page 832.

authorities.[31] In the case of H, however, the court considered an application by a local authority for a care order in a case involving six children. Recognising that the making of an order would allow the local authority to remove the children from the family, the court refused to do so. Thorpe LJ said that the court must consider Article 8 and the rights of both the family and the children of the family. In particular a judge:

> must not sanction such an interference with family life unless he is satisfied that that is both necessary and proportionate and that no other less radical form of order would achieve the essential end of promoting the welfare of the children.[32]

In this case the court accepted that the threshold for an interim care order was met, but the proportionate response was to adjourn the case for a short period without making an order.

Conclusions

In an article[33] Lady Hale has argued that the Human Rights Act 1998 has not greatly assisted in the development of economic and social rights in the mental health law field. Her opinion is based on a review of reported judicial decisions and related material. Whilst her analysis is authoritative it does not take into account, probably because it is impossible to quantify, the impact that human rights law has had on the changing approaches of professionals who work in this area. Over the last few years two particular groups of mental health professionals, section 12 approved doctors and ASWs, appear to be much more aware of the human rights issues that need to be considered when making problematic decisions in relation to children and young people. Looking at the problems of individual children and young people through a human rights 'prism' has provided clarity and focus in approaching the complex cases discussed in this book.[34]

---

31   W v. United Kingdom (1987) 10 EHRR 29.
32   Re B (Care: Inteference with Family Life) [2003] 2 FLR 813, page 821, paragraph 34.
33   Hale, B. 'The Human Rights Act and mental health law: has it helped?' Journal of Mental Health Law, May 2007, Northumbria Law Press, page 7.
34   '...while uncertainty remains regarding the extent to which practice will change in relation to minor's rights as a result of the Human Rights Act, such rights are increasingly seen as an important matter for debate and re-evaluation... It is conceivable therefore that as we become more accustomed to looking at a range of issues, such as health care, through the prism of human rights, views about parental authority over competent

Case examples

What human rights issues are raised by these case examples?

Donna is aged 15. She is demonstrating bizarre behaviour which is thought to be related to past trauma. With her agreement she is being treated in hospital. Her mother is not visiting her in hospital and will not consent to her treatment.

Manjula is aged 15. She is suffering from severe depression and a course of ECT is undertaken on the recommendation of the consultant child psychiatrist responsible for her treatment. She is not detained under the Mental Health Act and her parents have consented to her treatment.

Emma is being treated as an informal in-patient on an eating disorder unit. Sometimes she wants to be treated, at other times she is upset about the treatment that she says she is being forced to receive. When she is distressed she will try to leave the unit; she can usually be persuaded to stay although occasionally she will be prevented from leaving by the operation of an electronic key pass system. She is being treated on the basis of parental consent.

children will also undergo significant changes.' British Medical Association (2001) *Consent, Rights and Choices in Health Care for Children and Young People.* London: BMJ Books, page 9.

Chapter 2

The Children Act

Introduction

The main purpose of the Children Act 1989 was to bring together into a coherent whole a complex of laws that had developed over the years in a piecemeal fashion. Although the Act has been amended since 1989 (most importantly by the Adoption and Children Act 2002 and the Children Act 2004) the original framework remains intact. One of the primary aims of the Children Act at the time the Act was becoming operational was to strike:

> a balance between the rights of children to express their views on decisions made about their lives, the rights of parents to exercise their responsibilities towards the child and the duty of the state to intervene where the child's welfare requires it.[1]

The Children Act 1989 brings together both the 'private law' (governing legal relationships between private persons) and the 'public law' (governing legal relationships between private persons and the state) in relation to children.

The first part of this chapter focuses on one aspect of the Children Act 1989, parental responsibility. The exercise of parental responsibility intersects both private and public law insofar as a local authority (a social service authority) may acquire parental responsibility in the course of care proceedings. The second part deals with some of the legal principles and procedures that are common to both the private and public law. The third deals with private law, and the fourth deals with the public law provisions of the Children Act. This chapter is selective and does not contain a comprehensive

---

1   Department for Education and Skills (1991) *The Children Act 1989 Guidance and Regulations*, Volume 1. London: HMSO, paragraph 1.1.

overview of the Children Act, rather it identifies those areas of the law that will be of most relevance to CAMHS professionals. Other parts of the Children Act are dealt with elsewhere in this book: Chapter 8 deals with services for children and Chapter 3 deals with secure accommodation.

1 – Parental responsibility

What is parental responsibility?

The Children Act defines parental responsibility as follows:

> all the rights, duties, powers, responsibilities and authority which by law a parent of a child has in relation to the child and his property.[2]

The Act does not go any further in providing a list of the areas that fall within section 3. The courts have considered some aspects of parental responsibility and this includes consenting (or refusing to consent) to a child's medical treatment; this will include decisions about psychiatric treatment.

More than one person may have parental responsibility for the same child at any one time.[3] Where a local authority has a care order in respect of a child the local authority has parental responsibility for a child for the duration of the care order.[4] This does not extinguish any other persons' parental responsibility; it does mean that in the event of conflict between parent and local authority the authority may 'determine the extent to which a parent'[5] may meet his or her parental responsibility.

In relationship to the exercise of parental responsibility there are two specific provisions in the Children Act which are particularly significant to mental health professionals; these are sections 2(7) and 3(5).

SECTION 2(7)

> Where more than one person has parental responsibility for a child, each of them may act alone and without the other in meeting that responsibility.

---

2   Children Act 1989, section 3(1).
3   Ibid., section 2(5).
4   Ibid., section 33(3).
5   Ibid., section 33(3)(b).

This would, for example, cover the parent with whom the child lives making decisions about the child without having to consult, or obtain the consent of, the parent who is not living with the child. This would not prevent the other parent objecting but in the event of dispute it would be for the objecting parent to bring the matter to court.

SECTION 3(5)

This section provides that a person who does not have parental responsibility for a child but has care of the child may:

> do what is reasonable in all the circumstances of the case for the purpose of safeguarding or promoting the child's welfare.

This would cover, for example, a baby-sitter or a health care professional acting in an emergency if an accident were to happen to a child.

Who has parental responsibility?

THE MOTHER

Where a child's father and mother were not married to each other at the time of the child's birth the mother alone has parental responsibility.[6] The mother can lose parental responsibility when an adoption order is made in respect of a child. This will vest the adopters with parental responsibility and extinguish all other persons' parental responsibility.

THE FATHER

If the father was not married to the child at the time of the child's birth he may acquire parental responsibility by:

- becoming registered on the birth certificate (after 1.12.03)
- making a parental responsibility agreement with the mother
- court order (parental responsibility agreement or residence order).

Where the child's parents were not married at the time of the birth the child's father will acquire parental responsibility by subsequent marriage.[7]

---

6   Ibid., section 2(2)(a).
7   Legitimacy Act 1976, section 2.

OTHERS

Step-parents

A step-parent may acquire parental responsibility by either the child's parents (or parent if only one has parental responsibility) making an agreement with the step-parent or an order being made by the court on the application of the step-parent.[8]

Special guardian

The Adoption and Children Act 2002 introduced special guardianship to accommodate the type of cases where adoption was not suitable, for example where there were religious or cultural objections to the adoption process.

The effect of a special guardianship order is that the special guardian is entitled to exercise parental responsibility to the exclusion of any other person who has parental responsibility for a child.[9]

This list is not exhaustive. A local authority will acquire parental responsibility under a care order (see above) and, with restrictions, under an emergency protection order (EPO – see below). Where a residence order is made in favour of a person who is not the person's parent or guardian, that person will acquire parental responsibility during the continuance of the order.[10] Guardians may be appointed by parents with parental responsibility to take on parental responsibility for the parents' child on their death.

2 – Children Act principles

Section 1 of the Children Act, under the general heading of 'the welfare of the child', contains:

The welfare principle

This states (in summary) that when a court determines any question with respect to the upbringing of a child the child's welfare shall be the court's paramount consideration.[11]

The welfare principle is sometimes referred to as having application outside court proceedings in relation to children. This is incorrect as the

---

8   Children Act, section 4A(1), as amended by Adoption and Children Act 2002, section 112, and as amended by Civil Partnership Act 2004, section 75(1).
9   Children Act 1989, section 14A(1).
10   Ibid., section 12(2).
11   Ibid., section 1(1).

principle only has application to decisions made by the court in the context of either public or private law proceedings. Where protective steps are taken in relation to children outside court proceedings, section 3(5) of the Children Act (see below) will apply. The common law will have application: a doctor may lawfully treat a child in an emergency even though he is unable to obtain a valid consent. In exceptional cases, emergency treatment can be provided in the face of parental opposition.

> I accept that where there is no time to obtain a decision from the court, a doctor may safely carry out treatment in an emergency if the doctor believes the treatment to be vital to the survival or health of an infant and notwithstanding the opposition of a parent or the impossibility of alerting the parent before the treatment is carried out.[12]

The best interests of the child should always be a consideration. (See guidance to mental health professionals working with children and young people which advises that 'the best interests of the child and young person must always be considered'.)[13]

Delay prejudicial to welfare

Any delay in determining any question with regard to the upbringing of the child is likely to prejudice the welfare of the child.[14]

There may, however, be circumstances where the court will recognise that 'planned and purposeful delay' may be in the interests of the child.[15]

The welfare checklist

Section 1 contains a requirement that when making orders (this will cover most public and private law orders) the court must have regard to a statutory checklist. 'The list is not intended to be comprehensive, and is more of an aide-memoire for courts to ensure that the basic elements of a child's welfare are considered.'[16]

---

12   Lord Templeman in *Gillick* v. *West Norfolk and Wisbech Area Health Authority and another* [1985] 3 All ER, page 432.
13   Department of Health (2007) *Draft revised Mental Health Act 1983 Code of Practice*. London: DH, paragraph 39.9.
14   Children Act, section 1(2).
15   *C* v. *Solihull MBC* [1993] 1 FLR 290.
16   Hershman, D. and McFarlane, A. (2007) *Children, Law and Practice*. Family Law B-49 [201].

The welfare checklist

- The ascertainable wishes and feelings of the child (considered in the light of his age and understanding).

- His physical, emotional and educational needs.

- The likely effect on him of any change in his circumstances.

- His age, sex, background and any characteristics of his which the court considers relevant.

- Any harm which he has suffered or is at risk of suffering.

- How capable each of his parents, and any other person in relation to whom the court considers the question to be relevant, is of meeting his needs.

- The range of powers available to the court in the proceedings in question.

Apart from the last bullet point, the list could be used by mental health professionals to assist in the structuring of decision making in complex cases.

Where the court is making a decision in relation to the adoption of a child, the Adoption and Children Act 2002 requires the court to have regard to a modified checklist.

Court procedures

WHICH COURT?

Private law proceedings may be commenced in any court. Subject to certain exceptions most public law cases must be commenced in the family proceedings court (magistrates courts). Cases may be transferred to the county court, with the criteria for transfer including whether the proceedings are 'exceptionally grave, important or complex'.[17] The county court may make a decision that the case should be transferred to the High Court.

---

17   Children (Allocation of Proceedings) Order 1991.

THE CHILDREN'S GUARDIAN

A court considering any question with respect to a child under the Children Act 1989 may request a report on matters relating to the welfare of that child.[18] In practice this means that in the public law Children Act proceedings that are likely to involve mental health professionals (applications for care orders and secure accommodation orders) a children's guardian, formerly known as a guardian ad litem, will be involved. In private law proceedings a children and family reporter/welfare officer will be involved. Both guardian and welfare officer are managed by the Children and Family Court Advisory and Support Service (CAFCASS).

3 – Private law proceedings

In private law matters relating to children and young people four types of order can be made under section 8 of the Children Act. These orders are known as section 8 orders and are as follows.

Contact order

A contact order requires the person with whom a child lives, or is to live, to allow the child to visit or stay with the person named in the order, or for that person and the child otherwise to have contact with each other.

These orders will be made where there are disputes between separated parents over contact to their children.

Prohibited steps order

A prohibited steps order requires that no step which could be taken by a parent in meeting his parental responsibility for a child, of a kind specified in the order, shall be taken by any person without the consent of the court.

A prohibited steps order may prohibit a particular person having contact with a child or prohibiting the removal of a child from the jurisdiction.

---

18   Children Act 1989, section 7(1).

Residence order

A residence order settles the arrangements to be made as to the person with whom a child is to live.

A residence order can be made in favour of more than one person and may provide for the child to live with one person at one time and other people at other times. A residence order may be made in favour of any person, for example a grandmother. A residence order always gives parental responsibility for the child to any person in whose favour it is made.

Specific issue order

A specific issue order is an order giving directions for the purpose of determining a specific question which has arisen, or which may arise, in connection with any aspect of parental responsibility for a child.

If there is one specific disputed issue, for example in relation to the medical treatment of a child, the court can grant a specific issue order. For example, the court made an order authorising specific treatments in relation to a ten-month-old child who was suffering from leukaemia; the order was necessitated by the fact that the parents of the child were Jehovah's Witnesses and were not able to compromise their beliefs to give consent to the treatment.[19]

Section 8 orders can be made in public law proceedings, whether or not the threshold criteria are satisfied, but they cannot be in force at the same time as a care order. For example, a local authority could apply for a specific issue order in relation to an accommodated child where the authority is concerned about a particular aspect of the child's care.

4 – Public law proceedings

The duty to investigate – section 47 of the Children Act

Section 47 imposes duties on the local authority to investigate and 'make enquiries'. This duty arises in a number of circumstances including where a local authority is informed that a child, who lives or is found in its area, is:

---

19   *Re R (A Minor) (Blood Transfusion)* [1993] 2 FLR 757.

the subject of an emergency protection order; or is in police protection; or has contravened a ban imposed by a curfew order [under the Crime and Disorder Act 1998, section 14]; or has reasonable cause to suspect that a child who lives or is found in its area is suffering or likely to suffer significant harm.

In these circumstances the authority is required to make sufficient enquiries to enable it to decide whether it should take any action to safeguard or promote the welfare of the child. When determining what action to be taken, the local authority is required to ascertain the child's wishes and feelings.[21] The steps to protect and assist the child under the Children Act could include: implementing the procedures of the Act to protect children, initiating proceedings under section 31 and/or providing services under the Act.

Wardship and the inherent jurisdiction

Before the Children Act was implemented, the 'inherent jurisdiction' of the High Court was routinely used where there were disputes between parents and the local authority concerning decisions in relation to children. 'Wardship' was the machinery used to access the decision-making process. Following the implementation of the Children Act, the use of wardship dramatically declined. This was due to section 8 orders becoming available in private law proceedings, and in public law proceedings section 100 curtailed the powers of the High Court by preventing a child being both in care and a ward of court.[20]

Protecting children

Under the heading of 'Protection of Children' the Children Act contains provisions which include orders for EPOs and the powers of the police to 'remove and accommodate' children in emergencies. The police powers contained in the Act[22] are not court sanctioned and are time limited. A child can be kept in police protection for a maximum period of 72 hours.[23]

---

20   Children Act 1989, section 100(2)(c).
21   Children Act 1989, section 75(5A), as amended by Adoption and Children Act 2002.
22   Children Act 1989, section 46.
23   Ibid., section 46(6).

Public law orders

To protect children the court can make 'public law orders'. This term includes emergency protection orders, interim care orders, care orders and supervision orders. Orders can only be made if the 'threshold criteria' are met. These criteria are contained in section 31 of the Children Act.

The central concept of the criteria is whether there is harm, and if so whether it is significant. Harm is defined as ill-treatment or the impairment of health or development and includes sexual abuse and forms of ill-treatment which are not physical. The Adoption and Children Act 2002 extends the definition of harm by the addition of the clause 'including, for example, impairment suffered from seeing or hearing the ill-treatment of another'.[24] 'Health' means physical or mental health, and 'development' means physical, intellectual, emotional, social or behavioural development. The harm, or likelihood of harm, must be attributable either to the care given to the child 'not being what it would be reasonable to expect a parent to give' or to the child being beyond parental control.[25]

If a case is based on an allegation of actual significant harm, the court has to consider the question of whether the child was suffering significant harm at the time when the local authority acted to protect the child. The standard of proof in all children's cases is the balance of probabilities;[26] was the occurrence of the event more likely than not?

Even if the threshold criteria are satisfied, there remains a further step for the court to consider. The court must not make any order unless it considers that doing so would be better for the child than making no order at all.[27] All public law cases will involve the court having to consider fundamental human rights issues, in particular the application of Article 8, the right to respect for private and family life.

---

24   Adoption and Children Act 2002, section 120.
25   Children Act 1989, section 31(2)(b)(i) and (ii).
26   When assessing the probabilities the court will have in mind as a factor, to whatever extent is appropriate in the particular case, that the more serious the allegation the less likely it is that the event occurred and, hence, the stronger should be the evidence before the court concludes that the allegation is established on the balance of probability.' *Re H and R (Child Sexual Abuse: Standard of Proof)* [1996] 1 FLR 80.
27   *Re M (A Minor) (Care Order: Threshold Conditions)* [1994] 2 FLR 577.

Threshold criteria

This summary is adapted from Richard White's analysis in *Safeguards for Young Minds.*[28]

The criteria and the assessment required can be summarised as follows:

Step 1   Is the child suffering, or likely to suffer, harm by way of ill-treatment, impairment of health or impairment of development?

Step 2   If the harm suffered by a child is that of an effect on the child's health or development, then how does this child's health or development compare with that which could be reasonably expected of a similar child?

Step 3   Is this harm significant?

Step 4   Is this harm or its likelihood attributable to the care given to the child or likely to be given to him if the order were not made?

Step 5   Is the care given to the child not what it would be reasonable to expect a parent to give to him?

plus

Step 6   Would making an order be better for the child than making no order?

If an order is to be made what order would best protect the child?

What order would best meet the interests of the child?

(Consider the welfare checklist and remember that the welfare of the child is paramount.)

Evidential issues

CAMHS professionals are likely to be involved in two distinct parts of the court process. First, there may be significant concerns about the care a child is receiving from their parents. Translating those concerns into evidence suf-

---

28   White, R., Harbour, A. and Williams, R. (eds) (2004) *Safeguards for Young Minds*, 2nd edn. London: Gaskell, pages 29–32.

ficient to satisfy a court that the threshold criteria are met may require expert evidence as to, for example, psychological harm. Second, if the threshold criteria are met, evidence as to the care plan that would best meet the interests of the child may require evidence from a mental health professional. 'Split' hearings can take place: first proving the facts establishing the threshold and then, if the threshold is established, a second linked hearing will consider what order (if any) should be made.

In some cases the instinctive response of a CAMHS professional to a child's circumstances is to advocate that the child's interests require that the local authority have parental responsibility, under a care order, to control future decision making in relation to a child. Whilst this may appear to offer a solution to difficult cases, the evidential problems in establishing the criteria (significant harm) to justify asking the court to make a care order can be a costly, complex and time-consuming exercise.

Interim orders

The court can make an interim care or supervision order when adjourning an application. During the proceedings, and before a final order is made, a court can give directions to investigate a child's circumstances.[29] Where interim orders are made the court can direct the psychiatric examination and assessment of a child.[30]

If a child is 'of sufficient understanding to make an informed decision',[31] the child may refuse to submit to an examination or assessment. This 'statutory' right to refuse an assessment is largely illusory; in the case of *South Glamorgan County Council* v. *W and B* it was decided that the High Court in the exercise of its inherent jurisdiction can override the child's refusal to consent.[32]

Care order

The court can only make a care order if the threshold criteria are met. The care order gives parental responsibility to the local authority. Before a care

---

29   Children Act 1989, sections 37(1) and 38(1).
30   The scope of such court-directed assessments has been considered in *Re G (Interim Care Order: Residential Assessment)* [2004] 1 FLR 876.
31   Children Act 1989, section 38(6).
32   *South Glamorgan County Council* v. *W and B* [1993] 1 FLR 574.

order can be made the court has to be satisfied that the order is in the best interests of the child concerned:

> The court is under a duty rigorously to scrutinise the care plan advanced by the local authority, and if the court does not think that it meets the needs of the child concerned, the court can refuse to make a care order.[33]

Local authorities are under a duty to prepare a care plan for each child who is the subject of care proceedings.[34]

No care order may be made in respect of a child who has reached the age of 17, or 16 in the case of a married child.[35] A care order lasts until the child's 18th birthday unless it is brought to an end sooner.[36] A care order can be discharged in a number of ways including a successful application being made by a child, the local authority or a person with parental responsibility for the child.[37]

Contact with a child in care

Where a child is in the care of the local authority, the local authority must allow the child reasonable contact with persons including (this list is not comprehensive) his parents, guardian and a person under a residence order. A local authority may refuse contact if:

> they are satisfied that it is necessary to do so in order to safeguard or promote the child's welfare.[38]

If contact is refused then this can only be for a maximum of seven days without court sanction.[39]

---

33   *Re S and W (Care Proceedings)* [2007] 2 FLR 275, page 282, paragraph 27.
34   The Adoption and Children Act 2002 amends the Children Act 1989 and requires the local authority to prepare a care plan for 'the future care of the child'. Children Act 1989, section 31A. Guidance on the contents of a care plan in care proceedings are contained in Local Authority Circular LAC (99)29, 'Care Plans and Care Proceedings under the Children Act 1989' – see Appendix 2.
35   Children Act 1989, section 31(3). A care order will continue until a child is 18 unless ended earlier.
36   Ibid., section 91(2).
37   Ibid., section 39(4).
38   Ibid., section 34(6)(a).
39   Ibid., section 34(6)(b).

Supervision orders

If the threshold criteria are met then the court can make a supervision order. This order requires a local authority or probation officer to advise, assist and befriend a child. A supervision order does not confer parental responsibility on a local authority.

Where a court makes a supervision order (not an interim order) a requirement can be made that where the mental condition of the supervised child:

(a) is such as requires, and may be susceptible to treatment; but

(b) is not such as to warrant his detention in pursuance of a hospital order under Part III of that Act [the Mental Health Act 1983].[40]

The court may include in the order a requirement that the supervised child shall 'submit' to treatment. This could be treatment as a resident patient in a hospital. If the child is regarded as having 'sufficient understanding to make an informed decision'[41] the child's consent is required.

Conclusions

The person or persons with parental responsibility must be identified when a mental health professional has dealings with any child.[42] (The person with parental responsibility may not always be the parent.) Parents can provide authority to treat a child, and the provision of any medical treatment to a child without that authority may constitute an assault. The person with parental responsibility can provide consent on behalf of a child who is not 'Gillick competent'.[43] Even where a child is adjudged to be Gillick competent the law recognises that a child's refusal to be treated can, in certain circumstances, be overridden by a person with parental responsibility, or the court.

---

40   The Children Act 1989 specifies that a section 12 doctor must give evidence to justify an order being made under this section.
41   Children Act 1989, schedule 3, section 5(5)(a).
42   It is essential that those responsible for the care and treatment of the child or young person are clear about who has parental responsibility and always request copies of any court orders for reference on the child or young person's medical or social service file. These orders may include care orders, residence orders, contact orders, evidence of appointment as the child or young person's guardian, parental responsibility agreements or orders under section 4 of the Children Act and any order under wardship. Department of Health (2007) *Draft revised Mental Health Act 1983 Code of Practice*. London: DH, paragraph 38.39.
43   *Glass* v. *UK* [2004] 1 FLR 1019. For a discussion about the concept of Gillick competence see Chapter 12 and Appendix 3.

Under the Children Act, CAMHS professionals may be involved with children at two distinct stages. First, before protective proceedings have commenced they may be working with a child where harm is suspected.

> As part of assessment and care planning, child and adolescent mental health professionals should identify whether child abuse or neglect, or domestic violence, are factors in a child's mental health problems, and should ensure that this is addressed appropriately in the child's treatment and care. If mental health professionals think a child is currently affected, they should follow the child protection procedures laid down for their services within their area.[44]

Second, if proceedings have been commenced they may then be involved as both assessors and expert witnesses. Both situations require an up-to-date knowledge of the statutory framework surrounding the protection of children.

Case examples

> CAMHS professionals are providing therapeutic treatment to an 11-year-old boy, D. He lives with his mother. His father (who has parental responsibility) has had little contact with him. Without warning D's father writes to the psychologist in charge of D's treatment stating that the treatment must stop immediately as he does not consider it to be in D's interests.

> *What steps should the professionals take?*

> SP is aged 15. She is an only child. She has mild learning difficulties. She has been treated in hospital under section 3 of the Mental Health Act 1983, following a suicide attempt. She has been diagnosed as suffering from a depressive illness. Her depression is now controlled by medication, but unless someone reminds her she often forgets to take the medication. Those responsible for her care believe that, without medication, she will quickly become suicidal again. Before her admission to hospital SP was living with her parents. SP can return home, and she wants to go back there to live. However, her care coordinator suspects that SP may have been abused by her father.

> *What steps could be taken to protect SP?*

---

44   Department for Education and Skills (2006) *Working Together to Safeguard Children: A Guide to Inter-agency Working to Safeguard and Promote the Welfare of Children.* London: TSO, paragraph 2.89.

Chapter 3

Secure Accommodation

Introduction

Guidance was published in 1991 to accompany the implementation of the Children Act 1989. This guidance explains the reasons that section 25 of the Children Act was extended to cover not only the restriction of liberty of children 'looked after'[1] by the local authority but also to include children accommodated by health and local education authorities and children in private psychiatric hospitals.[2]

> Since 1983 local authorities have been precluded from placing children in their care in secure accommodation unless statutory criteria have applied, and moreover have been required to seek the authority of the court to continue such placements beyond a period of 72 hours. Children in a variety of other settings, however, have had no such statutory protection. For this reason the opportunity has been taken to extend the same statutory controls, which currently apply to local authority placements, to children accommodated by health and local education authorities, or accommodated in residential care, nursing or mental nursing homes.[3]

This underlines the importance of statutory protection being in place for all children and young people in a variety of settings where their liberty is being restricted.

---

1   The Children Act 1989 defines a looked-after child as either a child in the care of the local authority or a child provided with accommodation by the local authority. Children Act 1989, section 22(1)(a) and (b).
2   Children (Secure Accommodation) Regulations 1991, regulation 7(1)(a) and (b).
3   *The Children Act 1989 Guidance and Regulations* (1991), Volume 4. London: HMSO, paragraph 8.2.

Section 25 of the Children Act has similarities with the Mental Health Act 1983 (MHA), only insofar as both statutory regimes provide lawful authority for the restriction or deprivation of a child's liberty. The statutory provisions require that certain criteria have to be met before orders are made and that the justification for orders being made is reviewed by 'courts'. (Mental Health Review Tribunals are courts in the context of Mental Health Act detention.) Orders, if made, are time limited. Not too much should be made of these similarities; in the civil sphere the purpose of Mental Health Act detention is to allow for the compulsory treatment of a person's mental disorder within a statutory framework providing specific safeguards. The primary purpose of a secure accommodation order is to set out the conditions under which a child can be placed and kept in secure accommodation. Section 25 does not provide any authority to provide medical treatment to a child. (Compare with Part 4 of the Mental Health Act.)

There will be some young people who will move between the criminal justice system and in-patient psychiatric care. Some of those young people having been subject to secure accommodation orders will then be subject to Mental Health Act detention, and vice versa. This may give the impression that some choice has been exercised about the statutory regime that best meets the interests of the child. In reality the determination is generally made on the basis of a number of factors, most of which will be unplanned, for example the availability of a suitable resource at a particular time.

The application of the European Convention on Human Rights (ECHR) to secure accommodation orders is considered in the chapter on human rights, Chapter 1.

Restriction of liberty without court order

The maximum period during which a child's liberty may be restricted without the authority of a court is 72 hours, either consecutively or in aggregate in any period of 28 days.[4] This will apply to children accommodated by health and local education authorities and children in private psychiatric hospitals.

---

4   Children (Secure Accommodation) Regulations 1991, regulation 10(1).

Court proceedings

For any period beyond 72 hours the court must authorise a child being kept in secure accommodation. 'Court' means a youth or magistrates court in criminal proceedings or the family proceedings court in non-criminal proceedings. (If the child is already involved in care proceedings before the county court or High Court then application should be made to the court dealing with the case.)

A children's guardian will be appointed in civil proceedings but there is no provision for the youth or adult magistrates court to appoint a children's guardian.

Family proceedings

Secure accommodation may not be used in respect of a child unless it appears:

that he has a history of absconding and is likely to abscond from any other type of accommodation; and that if he absconds, he is likely to suffer significant harm; or that if he is kept in any other type of accommodation he is likely to injure himself or other persons.[5]

Criminal proceedings

The criteria applied by the court in family proceedings are modified in the case of children looked after by local authorities who are:

detained by the police and transferred to local authority accommodation; or refused bail and remanded to local authority accommodation under the Children and Young Persons Act 1969, who are charged with, or convicted of a violent or sexual offence, or of an offence punishable, in the case of an adult, with imprisonment for a term of 14 years or more; or the child has a recent history of absconding while remanded to local authority accommodation, and is charged with, or

---

5   Children Act 1989, section 25(1)(a) and (b).

convicted of an imprisonable offence alleged, or found to have been committed while he was so remanded.[6]

The modified criteria are that secure accommodation may not be used unless it appears that any accommodation other than that provided for the purpose of restricting liberty is inappropriate because:

the child is likely to abscond from such other accommodation; or the child is likely to injure himself or other people if he is kept in other accommodation.

Definition of secure accommodation

Secure accommodation is described in the Children Act as 'accommodation provided for the purpose of restricting liberty'.[7] This phrase covers both purpose-built units run by local authorities and psychiatric units run by health authorities where the regime is clearly intended to restrict the liberty of children.[8] It also covers other places which are not necessarily designed as secure accommodation.

Cazalet J held that a maternity ward secured by a key pass system fell within the definition of secure accommodation. In this case the young person who was the subject of the proceedings (DB) was 17 and had recently given birth to a child. She was a crack-cocaine addict and after the birth of her child it was decided that her best interests required her to be treated; she was not regarded as being competent. Nursing staff were instructed to prevent her from leaving the ward so that her life and health were not seriously endangered.

It is important to note that it is the restriction of liberty which is considered to be the essential factor in determining what is secure accommodation. To constitute secure accommodation, a place does not have to be so designated; each case will turn on its own facts.[9]

On the basis that DB was not competent, Cazalet J also authorised the use of reasonable force: 'to implement such medical treatment to DB as may be

---

6   Children (Secure Accommodation) Regulations 1991, regulation 6.
7   Children Act 1989, section 25(1).
8   R v. Northampton Juvenile Court ex parte London Borough of Hammersmith and Fulham [1985] FLR 193.
9   A Metropolitan Borough Council v. DB [1997] 1 FLR 767, page 774.

considered necessary by the doctors concerned for her to prevent her death or serious deterioration in her health'.[10]

In the same year Thorpe J held that a private psychiatric hospital specialising in eating disorder treatment 'was not designed for, or having as its primary purpose', the restriction of liberty.[11]

Whilst recognising that the interpretation of the term 'secure accommodation' was ultimately a matter for the court, guidance states:

> It is important to recognise that any practice or measure which prevents a child from leaving a room or building of his own free will may be deemed by the court to constitute restriction of liberty. For example, while it is clear that the locking of a child in a room, or part of a building, to prevent him leaving voluntarily is caught by the statutory definition, other practices which place restrictions on freedom of mobility (for example, creating a human barrier) are not so clear cut.[12]

On the other hand, measures to ensure the safety of a child would not necessarily constitute a restriction of liberty for the purposes of section 25. Guidance on permissible forms of control in children's residential care suggests:

> Homes should adopt normal domestic approaches to security, including, for example, the locking of all external doors at night.[13]

Who can apply for a secure accommodation order?

Applications to court for authority to use secure accommodation may only be made by or on behalf of a local authority looking after a child or, where the child is accommodated by a health authority or NHS trust, by that authority.[14]

---

10   *A Metropolitan Borough Council* v. *DB* [1997] 1 FLR 767, page 777.

11   *Re C (Detention: Medical Treatment)* [1997] 2 FLR 180.

12   *The Children Act 1989 Guidance and Regulations* (1991), Volume 4. London: HMSO, paragraph 8.10.

13   Department of Health (1993 *Guidance on Permissible Forms of Control in Children's Residential Care.* Local Authority Circular (LAC) (93)13. London: DH, paragraph 8.4.

14   Children (Secure Accommodation) (No 2) Regulations 1991.

The duty to avoid placing children in secure accommodation

Local authorities are under a duty to take reasonable steps to avoid placing children within their area in secure accommodation.[15] Guidance states:

> Restricting the liberty of children is a serious step which must be taken only when there is no appropriate alternative. It must be a 'last resort' in the sense that all else must first have been comprehensively considered and rejected – never because no other placement was available at the relevant time, because of inadequacies in staffing, because the child is simply being a nuisance or runs away from his accommodation and is not likely to suffer significant harm in doing so, and never as a form of punishment... Secure placements, once made, should be only for so long as is necessary and unavoidable. Care should be taken to ensure that children are not retained in security simply to complete a pre-determined assessment or 'treatment' programme.[16]

The length of the order

Initially, the maximum period of an authorisation is three months. The court should not automatically make an order for three months but must consider what is necessary in the circumstances of the case. 'The order should be for no longer than is necessary and avoidable.'[17] Authorisation may be renewed for further periods of up to six months at a time.[18]

A local authority, and this principle would also apply to a health authority, can only lawfully keep a child in secure accommodation for the maximum period specified in an order and whilst the criteria are still satisfied. It was held that a local authority who had accepted that the criteria for a secure order no longer applied but chose not to discharge a child until the expiry of the order acted unlawfully.[19]

---

15   Children Act 1989, schedule 2, paragraph 7.
16   *The Children Act 1989 Guidance and Regulations* (1991), Volume 4. London: HMSO, paragraph 8.5.
17   *Re W (A Minor) (Secure Accommodation Order)* [1993] 1 FLR 692.
18   Children (Secure Accommodation) Regulations 1991, regulation 12.
19   *LM* v. *Essex County Council* [1999] 1 FLR 988.

Minimum age

A child under the age of 13 years shall not be placed in secure accommodation in any children's home without the prior approval of the Secretary of State. If it appears likely that a section 25 order is going to be needed then contact with the Department of Health should be made as early as possible.

Interrelationship between the MHA and section 25

Section 25 shall not apply to a child who is detained under any provision of the Mental Health Act 1983.[20] If the child is subject to an order under section 2, but is not being detained because the child is on section 17 leave, then an application can be made for a secure accommodation order.[21]

The accommodated child

Local authorities are under a duty to provide accommodation for children in need. Section 20 of the Children Act 1989,[22] under the heading 'provision of accommodation for children: general', provides that:

> (3) Every local authority shall provide accommodation for any child in need within their area who has reached the age of sixteen and whose welfare the authority consider is likely to be seriously prejudiced if they do not provide him with accommodation.

> (4) A local authority may provide accommodation for any child within their area (even though a person who has parental responsibility for him is able to provide him with accommodation) if they consider that to do so would safeguard or promote the child's welfare.

> (5) A local authority may provide accommodation for any person who has reached the age of sixteen but is under twenty-one in any community home which takes children who have reached the age of sixteen if they consider that to do so would safeguard or promote his welfare.

---

20 Children (Secure Accommodation) Regulations 1991, regulation 5(1).
21 *Hereford and Worcester County Council* v. *S* [1993] 2 FLR 360.
22 Children Act 1989, section 20(3)–(5).

A young person over 16 who is being accommodated under section 20(5) of the Children Act cannot have their liberty restricted under section 25.[23] This does not mean that all children over 16 who are accommodated are precluded from being subject to a secure accommodation order; only young people accommodated at the local authority's discretion under section 20(5) are covered. So, for example, where the local authority has a duty to accommodate a child under section 20(3) that young person could be subject to a secure accommodation order.[24] Where a child is accommodated:

> Any person with parental responsibility for a child may at any time remove the child from accommodation provided by or on behalf of the local authority.[25]

This means that where a child or young person is accommodated (and not subject to a care order) and is also subject to a secure accommodation order then the person or persons with parental responsibility can remove the child or young person from secure accommodation. If, however, a person with a residence order, or a special guardianship order, agrees to the child being in secure accommodation then this provision will not apply.[26]

The application of the welfare principle in court proceedings

The court will take into account the child's welfare before making a secure accommodation order. The requirements of section 1 of the Children Act 1989, in particular the child's welfare being the court's paramount consideration, do not, however, have full application.[27]

Control and restraint of children

In general terms the control and restraint of children in children's homes is covered by regulations:

---

23   Children (Secure Accommodation) Regulations 1991, regulation 5(2)(a).
24   Re G (Secure Accommodation) [2000] 2 FLR 259.
25   Children Act 1989, section 20(8).
26   Ibid., section 20(9).
27   Re M (Secure Accommodation Order) [1995] 1 FLR 418.

No measure of control, restraint or discipline which is excessive, unreasonable or contrary to paragraph (5) [which lists a range of prohibited disciplinary measures including corporal punishment] shall be used at any time on children accommodated in a children's home.[28]

There is also some guidance adding substance to these regulations.[29] Although this guidance is expressly limited to children living in secure and open children's homes it must also have application to children in psychiatric hospitals. A summary of the lawful use of physical restraint includes the following pointers:

1. Staff should have good grounds for believing that immediate action is necessary to prevent a child from significantly injuring himself or others, or causing serious damage to property.

2. Staff should take steps in advance to avoid the need for physical restraint, for example through dialogue and diversion; and the child should be warned orally that physical restraint will be used unless he desists.

3. Only the minimum force necessary to prevent injury or damage should be applied.

4. Every effort should be made to secure the presence of other staff before applying restraint. These staff can act as assistants and witnesses.

5. As soon as it is safe, restraint should be gradually relaxed to allow the child to regain self-control.

6. Restraint should be an act of care and control, not punishment.

7. Physical restraint should not be used purely to force compliance with staff instructions when there is no immediate risk to people or property.

The age and competence of the child must always be taken into account when any measure involving control and restraint is being considered.

---

28   Children's Homes Regulations 2001, regulation 17(1).
29   Department of Health (1993) *Guidance on Permissible Forms of Control in Children's Residential Care*. LAC (93)13. London: DH, paragraph 5.6.

Conclusions

The provision of section 25 does not only apply to young people in purpose-built secure accommodation units managed by the local authority. Where the condition of a young person being treated as an informal patient in a psychiatric unit deteriorates, that may necessitate the use of restraint, 'time out' or other methods of control. If these interventions by necessity become more frequent and intense then restriction of liberty falling within section 25 may be taking place. Unless these restrictions fall within 'ordinary acceptable parental restrictions upon the movements of a child'[30] then authorisation will be required under either the Children Act, or the Mental Health Act or court order under the wardship/inherent jurisdiction.

Case example

V is aged 16. Her behaviour appeared to deteriorate about three years ago. Her parents are separated. She will not speak to her mother and she does not want to live with her father. She has been living with a friend and the friend's father. Over the last two years she has taken a number of overdoses of prescription drugs which have resulted in her admission to A&E. Her alcohol intake has increased resulting in her being arrested on a number of occasions. She has recently been the victim of a serious assault. She is known to CAMHS and the youth offending team. She is now being assessed at the general hospital following her admission and treatment for another overdose. Her behaviour is so disturbed she is being 'specialled' by three nurses at all times with the door to her room having to be locked.

V is not a risk to others – she is however vulnerable and chaotic. Does this mean she cannot be sectioned? If the Mental Health Act could be used what would be the grounds? Is it correct that because she is 16 the Children Act does not allow her liberties to be removed?

---

30   *Re K (Secure Accommodation Order: Right to Liberty)* [2001] 1 FLR 526.

Chapter 4

The Mental Health Act – Professionals, Relatives, Safeguards and Mental Disorder

Introduction

The Mental Health Act 1983 (MHA) consolidates the law in relation to mentally disordered persons. It is a comprehensive and sometimes confusing statute, which covers many aspects of the compulsory care and treatment of persons with mental disorder.[1] It also provides for the informal admission of patients.

The Mental Health Act 1983 is divided into various parts, for example Part 2 deals with 'civil' sections, Part 3 contains the sections relating to mentally disordered offenders and Part 4 provides a comprehensive framework for the treatment of patients detained under Parts 2 and 3.

This chapter covers the principles, framework and professional roles in the Mental Health Act 1983. Chapter 5 deals with the processes of admission, detention and discharge. The provisions relating to mentally disordered offenders are set out in summary form in Chapter 6.

Detention under the Mental Health Act 1983 has no lower or upper age limits. Only the guardianship and supervised after-care provisions are limited to those over the age of 16. It is possible, therefore, for children and

---

1   The Mental Health Act 1983 provides for the 'reception, care and treatment of mentally disordered patients, the management of their property and other related matters' (section 1(1)).

young people of any age to be compulsorily detained and treated under the Mental Health Act 1983. In practice, the majority of children admitted to psychiatric hospitals and units are admitted as informal patients and are covered by section 131.

This chapter, and Chapters 5 and 6, are based on the following material: statutes (the Mental Health Acts 1983 and 2007), statutory instruments (Mental Health (Hospital, Guardianship and Consent to Treatment) Regulations 1983 and the Mental Health Review Tribunal Rules 1983) and the Mental Health Act Code of Practice.[2] The Code's status is as follows:

> It is *guidance* not instruction…but it is much more than mere advice which an addressee is free to follow or not as it chooses. It is guidance which any hospital should consider with great care, and from which it should depart only if it has cogent reasons for doing so.[3]

In October 2007 a draft revised Mental Health Act 1983 Code of Practice[4] was published for consultation. This draft is referred to in the text as the 2007 Draft Code. The Mental Health Act 2007 requires the Code to include a statement of guiding principles. These principles apply equally to patients of all ages, but the chapter on children and young people contains further principles that have particular application to this age group.

Hospital managers

Formal responsibility for ensuring that detained patients are dealt with in accordance with the provisions of the Mental Health Act 1983 rests with the managers of the hospital.[5] The Act imposes a number of statutory functions on managers, for example to refer a patient's case to the Mental Health Review Tribunal. These functions may be delegated. The managers of many hospitals appoint a 'Mental Health Act administrator' to perform most of the

---

2   Department of Health (1999) *Mental Health Act 1983 Code of Practice.* London: DH. The Code was last revised in April 1999. Some parts of it have been rendered incorrect through judicial rulings since publication – see MHAC guidance (Oct 2005), www.mhac.org.uk (accessed 17.12.07).

3   Bingham LJ in *R* v. *Ashworth Hospital Authority (now Mersey Care NHS Trust) ex parte Munjaz* [2005] MHLR 276.

4   Department of Health (2007) *Mental Health Act 1983 Draft revised Code of Practice.* London: DH.

5   Both 'hospitals' and 'managers' are defined in section 145(1) of the Mental Health Act 1983.

statutory functions conferred by the Act and a panel of 'Mental Health Act managers' to deal with orders for discharge.

Professionals involved with the assessment and detention of patients

Approved social worker (ASW)

The MHA imposes a duty on the ASW to make an application for admission to hospital (or guardianship):

> ...in any case where he is satisfied that such an application ought to be made and is of the opinion, having regard to any wishes expressed by relatives of the patient or any other relevant circumstances, that it is necessary or proper for the application to be made.[6]

Until the Mental Health Act 2007 comes into force, only qualified social workers with additional specialist training are eligible to become ASWs. Local authorities are required to provide sufficient ASWs to meet the needs of their area.[7] The Mental Health Act 2007 replaces the ASW with the approved mental health professional (AMHP), who will take on the existing functions of ASWs. (The role and function of the ASW/AMHP is considered in detail in Chapter 9.)

Doctors (the MHA refers to 'medical practitioners')

In relation to both section 2 and 3 admissions, the Mental Health Act 1983 contains requirements for two doctors to sign recommendations. At least one doctor is required to have special experience in the diagnosis or treatment of mental disorder and one should preferably have previous acquaintance with the patient.[8] The Act contains rules prohibiting doctors who have a financial interest in treating a patient (for example in the context of being involved in a private hospital) from being involved in a patient's admission under compulsion.

---

6   Mental Health Act 1983, section 13(1).
7   Local Authority Circular, LAC (93)(10).
8   Approval is accorded via accreditation schemes organised by health authorities. Accreditation does not correspond with consultant status. Mental Health Act 1983, section 12.

The 1999 Code lists the responsibilities of the assessing doctor which include making a decision whether the patient is suffering from mental disorder and specifically addressing the legal criteria for admission under the Mental Health Act 1983. Furthermore, the 1999 Code states that the doctor should 'ensure that, where there is to be an application for admission, a hospital bed will be available'.[9]

Section 131A Mental Health Act 1983

The Mental Health Act 2007 inserts section 131A into the Mental Health Act 1983. The section entitled 'Accommodation etc. for children' applies to any person under the age of 18 years who is either 'liable to be detained in a hospital' under the Mental Health Act or is admitted to, or remains in, a hospital as an informal patient. The amended section provides that:

- The managers of the hospital shall ensure that the patient's environment in the hospital is suitable, having regard to his age (subject to his needs).

- For the purpose of deciding how to fulfil this duty the hospital managers shall consult a person who appears to them to have knowledge or experience of cases involving patients who have attained the age of 18 years which makes him suitable to be consulted.

The implementation date of this section is 1 April 2010.

The responsible medical officer (RMO)

The RMO is in charge of the patient's treatment in hospital. RMO is defined as the 'registered medical practitioner in charge of the treatment of the

---

9   Department of Health (1999) *Mental Health Act 1983 Code of Practice*. London: DH, paragraph 2.22(d). Compare the wording of the 2007 Draft Code: 'Unless different arrangements have been agreed locally, it is for the doctors (or one of them) to take the necessary steps to secure a suitable hospital bed, where appropriate, not the applicant.' Department of Health (2007) *Mental Health Act 1983 Draft revised Code of Practice*. London: DH, paragraph 4.67.

patient'.[10] The term is often incorrectly applied to describe a doctor in charge of an informal patient's treatment; it only has application to patients who are liable to be detained under the Mental Health Act 1983.

The Mental Health Act 2007 replaces the RMO with the 'responsible clinician' and introduces a new category of practitioner, the 'approved clinician'. Responsible clinicians and approved clinicians may include social workers, psychologists, nurses and occupational therapists as well as doctors. Both the responsible clinician and the approved clinician have specified functions within the Act. The definition of the responsible clinician is the approved clinician with 'overall responsibility for the patient's case'.[11]

The nearest relative

Introduction

The nearest relative occupies a central position within the scheme of the Mental Health Act 1983. The continuing existence of the nearest relative within the statutory scheme underlines their importance as a counterpoint to the power of the state vis-à-vis the use of compulsion on the individual. In the area of children's rights the legal authority of parent is central, and so the juxtaposition and linkage of the rights of the nearest relative alongside the rights of the parent need to be carefully considered. The nearest relative is a creature of statute and their rights and responsibilities are entirely delineated by the MHA. By contrast, the Children Act largely leaves the scope of parental responsibility undefined.

Rights

The MHA confers certain powers on the nearest relative. These include the right to request an ASW's assessment of the need for their relative to be detained in hospital.[12] Additionally they have the right to be consulted (where practicable) before a section 3 is applied for and to be able to block the application, to apply for a patient's detention in hospital and to order the

---

10   Mental Health Act 1983, section 34(1).
11   Mental Health Act 2007, sections 9–12.
12   Ibid., section 13(4).

patient's discharge.[13] Restricted patients[14] (see Chapter 6 on mentally disordered offenders) do not have a nearest relative.[15]

Although the nearest relative is entitled to apply for the patient to be admitted to hospital, this right is seldom used.

> The ASW is usually the right applicant, bearing in mind professional training, knowledge of the legislation and of local resources, together with the potential adverse effect that an application by the nearest relative might have on the latter's relationship with the patient.[16]

The managers of a hospital are required to give certain information to the nearest relative including seven days' notice of the intended discharge of a patient. These disclosure provisions do not apply if the patient objects.[17]

Defining the nearest relative

The patient's nearest relative is normally determined by taking whoever appears first in a list of relatives. The nearest relative must be ordinarily resident in the UK, the Channel Islands or the Isle of Man unless the patient is not so ordinarily resident. If there is more than one person in the same category then the older of the two shall be 'preferred' to the other.[18] The list is as follows:

- husband or wife
- son or daughter
- father or mother
- brother or sister
- grandparent
- uncle or aunt
- nephew or niece.

---

13   To advise the nearest relative prior to making an application for discharge, the MHA allows the nearest relative to arrange a medical assessment of the patient. Mental Health Act 1983, section 24(1).
14   Patients detained under sections 37 and 41 of the Mental Health Act 1983.
15   *R (on the application of H)* v. *MHRT* [2000] MHLR 203.
16   Department of Health (1999) *Mental Health Act 1983 Code of Practice.* London: DH, paragraph 2.25, page 696. This wording is largely reproduced in the 2007 Draft Code.
17   Mental Health Act 1983, sections 132 and 133.
18   Ibid., section 26(3).

If a patient usually lives with or is cared for by a relative, then that relative becomes the patient's nearest relative. Another category of potential nearest relative is a person with whom the patient has been 'ordinarily residing for a period of not less than five years'.[19] (This person will come last on the list.) A person under the age of 18 cannot be a nearest relative unless they are the patient's spouse or parent.

The MHA 2007 amends the MHA 1983 Act and inserts civil partners (as defined by the Civil Partnership Act 2004) into the nearest relative provisions. These amendments were implemented on 1 December 2007.

Delegating the role of the nearest relative

Regulations[20] allow a nearest relative to authorise someone else to perform their functions. This other person need not be a relative defined by the MHA but must not fall within the list of persons excluded by the Act,[21] for example a person under the age of 18.

The nearest relative as parent

Where the person to be detained is a child or young person then it is likely that the nearest relative will be the child's parent. The elder parent generally will have parental responsibility for the child. If, however, the child's parents are separated then the parent with whom the child normally resides will be the nearest relative, even though that parent may be the younger of the two.[22]

The father with parental responsibility

The MHA provides that a father with parental responsibility may be the nearest relative.[23] (Chapter 2 details the law in relation to parental responsibility.)

---

19   Ibid., section 26(7).
20   Mental Health (Hospital, Guardianship and Consent to Treatment) Regulations 1983, regulation 14.
21   Mental Health Act 1983, section 26(5).
22   Ibid., section 26(4).
23   Ibid., section 26(2)(b).

The father without parental responsibility

How can the father of the child who does not have parental responsibility for that child become the child's nearest relative?

- The existing nearest relative has authorised his appointment in writing under Regulation 14.

- The court has appointed him to act following an application under section 26.

- The child patient has ordinarily resided with him and has done so for at least five years.

Can the child's father, who is prevented from being the child's nearest relative because he does not have parental responsibility, take on the role when the child becomes 18? The Mental Health Act 1983 does not appear to leave much room for manoeuvre in this situation:

> People whose parents were not married are regarded as related only to their mother's side of the family and not to their father unless he 'has' parental responsibility for them (s.26(2)); he cannot have this once the children are grown up, however close their relationship was or now is.[24]

The Mental Health Act 2007 provides another option which will be for the patient to apply to displace their existing nearest relative.

Displacement

If, following consultation, the nearest relative objects to a section 3 application being made, the application cannot go ahead unless the county court displaces the nearest relative and appoints an acting nearest relative. The Mental Health Act 1983 contains four grounds[25] for displacing a nearest relative. The grounds, quote directly from the Act, are:

a.   that patient has no nearest relative within the meaning of this Act, or that it is not reasonably practicable to ascertain whether he has such a relative, or who that relative is;

b.   that the nearest relative of the patient is incapable of acting as such by reason of mental disorder or other illness;

24   Hoggett, B. (1996) *Mental Health Law*, 4th edn. London: Sweet & Maxwell, page 55.
25   Mental Health Act 1983, section 29.

c. that the nearest relative of the patient unreasonably objects to the making of an application for admission for treatment or a guardianship application in respect of the patient; or

d. that the nearest relative of the patient has exercised without due regard to the welfare of the patient or the interests of the public his power to discharge the patient from hospital or guardianship…or is likely to do so.

In relation to a refusal by a parent to the admission of their child under section 3, what is considered to constitute a reasonable objection may not always be clearcut.[26] For example, a parent may be supportive of all aspects of an in-patient treatment plan to treat a seriously ill child but may object to the use of the Mental Health Act 1983 on the grounds that the use of the Act would stigmatise the child.

The Mental Health Act 2007 introduces a new ground for displacement: the nearest relative is unsuitable to act. The effect of this amendment will be to allow, for example, an AMHP to apply on behalf of a child patient for the appointment of another nearest relative where it is alleged that the patient's father (who is also the nearest relative) has abused the patient.

If the court chooses to appoint a nearest relative under ground a. above, or displaces a nearest relative under grounds b., c. or d. above, then the court may appoint the applicant for the order as nearest relative or another person named in the application, for example another relative of the patient or a social worker.

The local authority as nearest relative

Where the child is in the care of the local authority under a care order the authority is:

deemed to be the nearest relative of the patient in preference to any person except the patient's husband or wife.[27]

---

26 The only detailed consideration given by the courts to reasonableness in this context was in 1973. In the *W* v. *L* case, Lord Denning stated that the proper test 'is to ask what a reasonable woman in her place [she was the nearest relative, the subject of displacement proceedings] would do in all the circumstances of the case'. *W* v. *L* [1973]3 All ER, page 889.

27 Mental Health Act 1983, section 27(a).

Care order includes interim care order.[28] The practical effect of the section must be to require social services departments to have in place a procedure for designating a senior manager to be able to adopt the role of the child's nearest relative.

Other persons with parental responsibility

Where a residence order is in force, or the child has a guardian (including a special guardian),[29] then the person named in the residence order is 'deemed to be the nearest relative'.[30] If there is more than one guardian, or person named under a residence order, the MHA appears to allow the adults involved to share the rights and responsibilities of being the nearest relative. (This is in contrast to the list referred to above where if there is more than one person in the same category, for example mother and father of the patient, then the oldest of the two will be the nearest relative.)

Wards of court

The MHA contains 'special provisions as to wards of courts'.[31] This includes the requirement that leave of the court is obtained before a child can be detained. As the Children Act has significantly curtailed the use of wardship, these provisions are seldom used.

Informal admission

The MHA provides for the informal admission of patients to hospital, and for patients who have been discharged from detention to remain in hospital informally. Section 131 specifically refers to children:

> In the case of a minor who has attained the age of 16 years and is capable of expressing his own wishes, and such arrangements [to admit or to remain in hospital] may be made, carried out and determined even

---

28   Ibid., section 31(11).
29   See Chapter 2 for the definition of special guardian.
30   Mental Health Act 1983, section 28(1).
31   Ibid., section 33.

though there are one or more persons who have parental responsibility for him within the meaning of the Children Act 1989.[32]

In the case of *R* v. *Kirklees Metropolitan Borough Council (MBC) ex parte C*,[33] a 12-year-old subject to a care order was admitted to a psychiatric hospital for an assessment. The lawfulness of the decision of the local authority acting 'in loco parentis' to consent to the decision was challenged. The court held (with the decision being upheld by the Court of Appeal) that as the child was regarded as not being 'Gillick competent' the local authority under a care order could consent to her admission. It is likely that a case with similar facts would be decided differently today as the application of section 25 of the Children Act, and the engagement of Article 5, would have to be considered.

The Mental Health Act 2007 amends section 131. The effect of this amendment is that if the young person (who must have capacity) consents to informal admission then that consent cannot be overridden by a person with parental responsibility for them. Conversely, if the young person (who again must have capacity) does not consent to admission they cannot be admitted informally on the basis of a person with parental responsibility consenting on their behalf. Instead, the young person will have to be detained, if the criteria are met.

If this section is to be relied on, a formal assessment of the capacity of the young person will need to be undertaken using the tests contained in section 3 of the Mental Capacity Act.

Definitions of mental disorder

Mental disorder is a legal classification that does not bear any precise relationship to medical diagnoses. In particular the legal classifications contained in section 1 of the Mental Health Act 1983 do not correspond with the diagnoses of mental disorder commonly applied to children, for example attention deficit hyperactivity disorder (ADHD) and post-traumatic stress disorder (PTSD). Mental disorder is defined in the Mental Health Act 1983 as 'mental illness, arrested or incomplete development of mind, psychopathic disorder and any other disorder or disability of mind'.[34]

---

32   Ibid., section 131(2).
33   *R* v. *Kirklees Metropolitan Borough Council ex parte C (QBD)* [1992] 2 FLR 117 and *R* v. *Kirklees Metropolitan Borough Council ex parte C (CA)* [1993] 2 FLR 187.
34   Mental Health Act 1983, section 1.

Section 131 of the Mental Health Act

The full text of section 131 of the Mental Health Act 1983 as amended by the Mental Health Act 2007 is as follows:

131. (1) Nothing in this Act shall be construed as preventing a patient who requires treatment for mental disorder from being admitted to any hospital or [registered establishment] in pursuance of arrangements made in that behalf and without any application, order or direction rendering him liable to be detained under this Act, or from remaining in any hospital or [registered establishment] in pursuance of such arrangements after he has ceased to be so liable to be detained.

(2) Subsections (3) and (4) below apply in the case of a patient aged 16 or 17 years who has capacity to consent to the making of such arrangements as are mentioned in subsection (1) above.

(3) If the patient consents to the making of the arrangements, they may be made, carried out and determined on the basis of that consent even though there are one or more persons who have parental responsibility for him.

(4) If the patient does not consent to the making of the arrangements, they may not be made, carried out or determined on the basis of the consent of a person who has parental responsibility for him.

(5) In this section –

(a) the reference to a patient who has capacity is to be read in accordance with the Mental Capacity Act 2005; and

(b) 'parental responsibility' has the same meaning as in the Children Act 1989.

The implementation date of this section 1 January 2008.

The Act contains four specific categories of mental disorder: mental illness, severe mental impairment, mental impairment and psychopathic disorder. Some Mental Health Act 1983 orders, for example section 2 or section 136, only require that the patient should be suffering from mental disorder. The longer-term orders require that the patient should be suffering from one of the four specified categories of mental disorder.

The Mental Health Act 2007 amends the wording of the definition of mental disorder to read 'any disorder or disability of the mind'. This is likely to have a significant impact on CAMHS. For example, young people who have been traditionally regarded as not being 'sectionable' may now be detained under the MHA providing the criteria are met.[35] The 2007 Code includes, in a list of 'clinically recognised conditions', 'behavioural and emotional disorders of children and adolescents',[36] which could fall within the definition of mental disorder. The Code then goes on to advise that:

> The Act therefore applies to personality disorders (of all types) in exactly the same way as it applies to mental illness and other mental disorders.[37]

A person cannot be dealt with or detained under the Mental Health Act 1983 as suffering from any form of mental disorder 'by reason only of promiscuity or other immoral conduct, sexual deviancy or dependence on alcohol or drugs'.[38]

The Mental Health Act 2007, when in force, will replace the exclusions contained in section 1(3) with a single exclusion: 'Dependence on alcohol or drugs is not considered to be a disorder or disability of mind.'[39] This means, for example, that there will be no grounds for detaining a young person on the grounds of drug dependence alone. If, however, this drug dependence is accompanied by another mental disorder then the use of the Act could be justified if the criteria were met.[40]

---

35   In *Re K (Secure Accommodation Order: Right to Liberty)* [2001] 1 FLR 526, page 529, paragraph 5, a 16-year-old with a diagnosis of 'hyperkinetic conduct disorder' was not considered to have mental illness or mental impairment under the Mental Health Act 1983.

36   Department of Health (2007) *Mental Health Act 1983 Draft revised Code of Practice*. London: DH, paragraph 3.3.

37   Ibid., paragraph 3.15.

38   Mental Health Act 1983, section 1(3).

39   Mental Health Act 2007 section 3.

40   Mental Health Act 1983, section 1(2).

Learning disabilities and the Mental Health Act 1983

Persons with learning difficulties currently only come within the Mental Health Act 1983 description of mental impairment if they have 'a state of arrested or incomplete development of mind' which is associated with 'abnormally aggressive or seriously irresponsible conduct'.[39]

The courts have adopted a restrictive approach to the concept of serious irresponsibility. In the case of F, a 17-year-old learning disabled child, she wanted to return home. The local authority regarded her as being at some risk if she did so. As the court regarded the urge to return home as 'almost universal' they concluded that F's determination could not be regarded as seriously irresponsible.[41]

Although the Mental Health Act 2007 introduces a single definition of mental disorder it provides that for certain sections of the Act (apart from section 2 and other short-term sections) a person may not be considered to be suffering from a mental disorder simply as a result of having a learning disability unless that disability is associated with abnormally aggressive or seriously irresponsible conduct on the part of the person concerned.

Treatability

At present the long-term detention of patients classified as suffering from either psychopathic disorder or mental impairment (as opposed to severe mental impairment) can only take place if they are 'treatable'. For the admission for treatment under section 3 (or a section 37 hospital order) of patients who come within these two categories of mental disorder, the treatment must be 'likely to alleviate or prevent a deterioration' of the condition. To justify the renewal of authority to detain a patient under a section 3 or 37, the treatability test must be applied to patients subject to all four categories of mental disorder; however, if the person does not pass this test at renewal, and suffers from mental illness or severe mental impairment, there is an alternative test of being 'unable to care for himself, to obtain the care which he needs or to guard himself against serious exploitation'.[42]

---

41   Re F (Mental Health Act: Guardianship) [2000] 1 FLR 192.
42   Mental Health Act 1983, section 20(4)(b) and (c).

The Mental Health Act 2007 replaces the 'treatability' test with an 'appropriate medical treatment' test.[43] Because of the abolition of the categories of mental disorder, the appropriate medical treatment test applies equally to all patients detained under sections 3 and 37. Section 3(4) as amended by the 2007 Act explains that the test requires the proposed medical treatment to be clinically appropriate for the nature and degree of the patient's mental disorder as well as other factors. The 2007 Draft Code lists a number of factors that are relevant in applying the test including whether 'age-appropriate accommodation'[44] is available.

Nature or degree

The distinction between 'nature' (the type of the disorder) and 'degree' (the severity of the disorder) is central to understanding the operation of the Mental Health Act 1983. The wording was considered by Popplewell J: 'The word nature refers to the particular mental disorder, its chronicity, its prognosis and the propensity of the patient to relapse; degree refers to the current manifestation of the illness.'[45]

By way of example, a patient with a bipolar disorder when first admitted under section to hospital is floridly ill; his illness therefore is both of a nature and degree warranting detention. Within a few weeks the symptoms of the illness have abated as a consequence of an effective treatment regime. At this point if there was evidence that his mental health would deteriorate if he did not take medication, and there was also evidence that he had been non-compliant in the past, the nature of his illness rather than the degree would justify his continuing detention.

---

43 The Mental Health Act 2007 amends the definition of medical treatment to include 'nursing, psychological interventions and specialist mental health habilitation, rehabilitation and care'. Reference to medical treatment in the Mental Health Act 1983 is also to be 'construed as a reference to medical treatment the purpose of which is to alleviate, or prevent a worsening of, the disorder or one or more of its symptoms or manifestations'. Mental Health Act 2007, section 7(1)–(3).

44 Department of Health (2007) *Mental Health Act 1983 Draft revised Code of Practice*. London: DH, paragraph 6.9.

45 *R* v. *MHRT for the South Thames Region ex parte Smith* [1999] COD 148.

Care and treatment of detained patients in hospital

The Mental Health Act 1983 is the only statute in England and Wales which deals comprehensively with provision of medical treatment[46] by providing a statutory framework for the provision of medical treatment for mental disorder where a patient refuses to give, or is incapable of giving, consent. The provisions for such compulsory treatment are set out in Part 4 of the Act. The provisions apply to most detained patients, in particular those detained under sections 2, 3 and 37.

Certain treatments may be given without either the consent of the patient or the involvement of the second opinion appointed doctor (SOAD) provided the treatment is for the patient's mental disorder. The SOAD is appointed by the Mental Health Act Commission (MHAC). The Mental Health Act 1983 provides that:

> The consent of a patient shall not be required for any medical treatment given to him for the mental disorder from which he is suffering, not being treatment falling within section 57 or 58 above, if the treatment is given by or under the direction of the responsible medical officer.[47]

Under section 63 no special procedures need be followed before the treatment can be imposed. Treatments for physical conditions may only be given under section 63 if such treatment is ancillary to the treatment for the patient's mental disorder; this would include treating the symptoms or the consequences of the mental disorder.[48] Treatments for anorexia nervosa and feeding by nasogastric tube fall within section 63.[49]

The limits to treatment under section 63 are not always easy to discern. In the case of C[50] Thorpe J decided that a patient detained under the MHA was entitled to refuse treatment for gangrene on the basis that the treatment for the gangrene 'was entirely unconnected with the mental disorder'. This case was distinguished by Wall J in the case of a pregnant patient detained

---

46   Medical treatment is defined in the Mental Health Act 1983, section 145(1), as: 'Medical treatment *includes* nursing, and also *includes* care, habilitation and rehabilitation under medical supervision.'

47   Mental Health Act 1983, section 63.

48   B v. *Croydon District Health Authority* [1995] 1 All ER 683 and R v. *Collins and Ashworth Hospital Authority ex parte Brady* [2000] MHLR 17.

49   *Riverside Health NHS Trust* v. *Fox* [1994] 1 FLR 614 and also MHAC Guidance Note 3 on Anorexia Nervosa (issued August 1992 and updated March 1999).

50   *Re C (Adult: Refusal of Medical Treatment)* [1994] 1 All ER 819.

under section 3 who was refusing a caesarean section. He decided that a caesarean section fell within section 63: 'It is not, therefore, stretching language unduly to say that achievement of a successful outcome of her pregnancy is a necessary part of the overall treatment of her mental disorder.'[51]

Section 57 of the Mental Health Act 1983 contains particular safeguards[52] for certain irreversible treatments including neurosurgery. The safeguards apply to both informal and detained patients. In summary, irreversible psychiatric treatments cannot be carried out without authorisation given by a panel of experts that is appointed by the Mental Health Act Commission and the valid consent of the patient is required.

Section 58 of the MHA provides safeguards in relation to two particular forms of treatment: medication after three months and ECT. Either valid consent needs to be obtained and recorded or a SOAD is needed.

- *Valid consent.* In this case the patient's consent needs to be recorded on a certificate which verifies the validity of this consent (Form 38). This certificate must be completed either by the RMO or by a SOAD who is appointed by the MHAC.

- *Refusal or incapacity.* In this case a certificate is needed, completed by a SOAD, stating that the treatment is appropriate (Form 39). Before signing, the doctor must consult with a nurse and with one other professional who is concerned with the patient's treatment. The staff who are consulted should make a record of this in the patient's notes.

The provision of urgent treatment to patients is covered in section 62 of the MHA. This disapplies the safeguards in place under sections 57 and 58 if certain criteria are met, including where treatment is immediately necessary to save a patient's life.[53]

The provision of ECT to children and young people is covered by new safeguards inserted into the Mental Health Act 1983 by the Mental Health Act 2007.[54] These safeguards apply to all patients under the age of 18 regardless of whether they are detained. Where a patient under 18 consents to ECT, a SOAD must certify both the consent and that it is appropriate for

---

51   *Tameside and Glossop Acute Services Trust* v. *CH* [1996] 1 FLR 762.
52   Mental Health Act 1983, section 57.
53   Ibid., section 62.
54   Mental Health Act 2007, section 58A.

the treatment to be given. Where a patient under 18 is not able to consent the treatment may be certified as appropriate by a SOAD.[55] Informal patients under 18 cannot be given ECT without a SOAD certificate. In relation to those under 18 who lack capacity the SOAD certificate does not by itself provide authority to give the treatment; there must be some other authority. This could be provided by someone with parental responsibility,[56] the court or, if the young person is aged over 16, under the provisions of the Mental Capacity Act.

Advocacy

Section 20 of the Mental Health Act 2007 inserts a new section, 130A, into the Mental Health Act 1983, requiring arrangements to be made to enable 'independent mental health advocates' to be available to help 'qualifying patients'. A qualifying patient will be one who is detained under most sections of the Act or who is subject to guardianship or a community treatment order.

The Mental Health Act Commission (MHAC)

The MHAC has a number of functions including: visiting and interviewing detained patients, investigating complaints that come within its jurisdiction and appointing SOADs for the purpose of providing a second opinion and verifying consent.

Complaints by or on behalf of a detained patient which are not resolved satisfactorily by the hospital can be referred to the MHAC to investigate. It is to be regretted that this aspect of the MHAC's remit does not extend to informal patients under section 131, particularly children who are admitted following the consent of a parent.

Until about ten years ago the MHAC consistently expressed serious concerns about the vulnerability of children and young people who were

---

55   Ibid., section 58A(7).
56   The 2007 Draft Code advises that either 'the child or young person must consent to it
       personally, or there must be some other lawful authority to give it, e.g. under the MCA for
       patients who are 16 or 17 years old'. Department of Health (2007) *Mental Health Act 1983
       Draft revised Code of Practice.* London: DH, paragraph 25.43.

informal patients, and in particular at the lack of safeguards available.[57] The MHAC's focus then shifted from the children who were 'de facto' detained to the uneven provision of service for seriously mentally ill children.[58]

Recent biennial reports[59] have in the main focused on the problems faced by children and young people who are admitted to adult units. The ninth biennial report (covering the period 1999–2001) presented data to show that, of 1082 children and young people admitted to hospital under the Mental Health Act 1983, 378 young men and 246 young women were admitted to adult wards. (The MHAC accepted that this data was likely to be affected by significant under-reporting.) The figure for admissions to adult facilities for both sexes were 138 in 2001–2 and 132 in 2002–3. The most recent data from the MHAC shows a total of 310 detained child and adolescent inpatients resident on 31 March 2007 within the NHS and independent sector.[60]

The MHAC is likely to be subsumed into a larger organisation within the relatively near future.

> The government has signalled its intention to bring forward a Bill to establish a new, integrated health and adult social care regulator, bringing together existing health and social care regulators, including the Mental Health Act Commission, into one regulatory body.[61]

Case examples

> G is a 17-year-old subject to a care order under the Children Act. Both his parents have regular contact with him and he is shortly to return home to live with them.
>
> *Who is his nearest relative under the Mental Health Act?*

---

57   The First Biennial Report of the MHAC, 1983–1985, page 12; the Second Biennial Report of the MHAC, 1985–1987, pages 50–51; the Fifth Biennial Report of the MHAC, 1991–1993, pages 56–57; and the Seventh Biennial Report of the MHAC, 1995–1997, pages 46–47.

58   The Seventh Biennial Report of the MHAC, 1995–1997, pages 187–188; the Eighth Biennial Report of the MHAC, 1997–1999, page 247.

59   The Ninth Biennial Report of the MHAC, 1999–2001, pages 72–73; the Tenth Biennial Report of the MHAC, 2001–2003, pages 245–253; and the Eleventh Biennial Report of the MHAC, 2003–2005, pages 132–133 and the Twelfth Biennial Report of the MHAC, 2005–2007, pages 134–138.

60   The Twelfth Biennial Report of the MHAC, 2005-2007, page 134.

61   Department of Health (2007) *Mental Health Act 1983 Draft revised Code of Practice*. London: DH, page 11.

K is a 17-year-old language student from Switzerland staying in England for a two-month course. She becomes unwell and is admitted to hospital under section 2. It is decided that she needs to be treated under section 3. She has several family members living in France and Switzerland.

Who is her nearest relative?

B is 15. He lives with his aunt under a special guardianship order made when he was 14. Both his parents are alive and have parental responsibility for him.

Who is his nearest relative?

A's mother died recently. He has a close relationship with his father. His father never acquired parental responsibility for A and does not live with, or care for, his son. A is now 19 and consideration is being given to admitting A to hospital under the MHA. There is no other person who could be considered to be A's nearest relative apart from his father.

Can the ASW regard A's father as his nearest relative?

L is aged 15. He has a history of behavioural difficulties, including offending. The offences are mainly property crimes. He abuses solvents and cannabis. He has been accommodated by social services at his mother's request on a number of occasions. His father recently committed suicide in prison. He was admitted to the local child and adolescent psychiatric unit following a disturbance at the family home. L was out of control, having smashed a window and having attempted to jump off the top of the block of flats where he lives. He has received in-patient treatment for a period of two weeks. He is now described as actively psychotic. He wants to leave hospital and is not compliant with the treatment regime in the unit. His mother, who is his nearest relative, is very supportive of the clinical team's efforts to contain him and agrees with his in-patient treatment plan. However, she does not believe that L should be detained, as that, in her words, 'would stigmatise him'.

Is L's mother's objection unreasonable?

Y is aged 16. She is described as suffering from a schizo-affective disorder. Because she presents a risk of absconding and harming herself, she has been admitted under section 2 of the Mental Health Act 1983 to the local mental health service's psychiatric intensive care unit. She is not compliant with any form of treatment. She is also refusing to eat in order to harm herself further.

What treatment can be given to her without her consent under the Mental Health Act 1983? Would the answer be any different if she was detained under section 3 of the Mental Health Act 1983?

Chapter 5

The Mental Health Act – Assessment, Detention, Treatment Discharge and Other Orders

Introduction

This chapter is in two parts. The first part deals with the processes in the Mental Health Act 1983 that apply to a person from the time that they are assessed as eligible to be detained to the time they are discharged. This chapter links with the preceding chapter: a person cannot be detained under the Mental Health Act 1983 unless there is evidence of mental disorder and a person cannot be compulsorily treated for mental disorder unless they are detained and covered by Part 4 of the Mental Health Act 1983 (which deals with the provision of medical treatment for mental disorder). The second part of the chapter deals with other orders under the Mental Health Act.

1 – From assessment to discharge

Holding powers

SECTION 5(2)

This section provides statutory authority to 'hold' an in-patient to allow that patient to be assessed for admission under the Mental Health Act 1983. The section lasts for a maximum of 72 hours and only applies to an in-patient in a hospital. The person exercising this power is the doctor in charge of the patient's treatment, or his or her nominee, who must believe that the person should be detained under section 2 or 3. The power could be used, for example, to hold a young person on a paediatric ward whilst a Mental Health Act 1983 assessment is undertaken and the paediatrician in charge of the child's treatment could furnish the necessary report. The procedure to be followed requires the doctor in charge of the patient's treatment to provide a report to the hospital managers setting down full reasons why informal treatment is no longer appropriate. Delivery of the report provides authority to detain the patient for a 72-hour period 'from the time the report is so furnished'.[1]

> Where a report under section 5(2) is provided in relation to a patient under the care of a consultant other than a psychiatrist, the doctor invoking the power should make immediate contact with a psychiatrist.[2]

A patient cannot be transferred to another hospital under section 5(2) and cannot be granted leave, even under escort.

SECTION 5(4)

This section allows nurses of prescribed levels of training to restrain, or authorise the restraint of, a patient, for a maximum period of six hours. Unlike section 5(2) above, this section only covers in-patients who are receiving treatment for mental disorder and can only be used if the patient is trying to leave hospital.

Admission for assessment (section 2)

A person of any age can be admitted to hospital and detained for up to 28 days. The application, to the managers of the hospital, may be made by the person's nearest relative or by an ASW. The ASW's responsibilities are discussed in Chapter 9. The provisions contained in the Mental Health Act 2007 relating to 'approved mental health professions' (AMHPs) will come into force on 1 October 2008. From that date onwards all references in this chapter to an ASW should be read as referring to AMHPs.

---

1   Mental Health Act 1983, section 5(2).
2   Department of Health (1999) *Mental Health Act 1983 Code of Practice*. London: DH, paragraph 8.6.

It was held in the case of *Williamson* that the use of successive or 'back to back' applications was unlawful.[3]

In relation to both section 2 and 3 admissions, the Mental Health Act 1983 contains requirements that the application must be based on the separate or joint recommendations of two doctors, one of whom, if practicable, must know the patient. At the time of writing, one of the doctors must be approved under section 12(2) of the Mental Health Act 1983 (but see note in Chapter 4 on 'approved clinicians' under the Mental Health Act 2007). Each doctor must have personally examined the patient. If the doctors examine the person separately, not more than five days[4] may elapse between the days on which the examinations take place.

The legal criteria for admission are that the patient:

- is suffering from mental disorder of a nature or degree which warrants the detention of the patient in hospital for assessment (or for assessment followed by medical treatment) for at least a limited period; and

- he ought to be so detained in the interests of his own health or safety or with a view to the protection of other persons.

Admission for assessment in cases of emergency (section 4)

The purpose of the section is to cover a patient's admission where the circumstances are sufficiently urgent to justify not waiting for a second doctor. The section lasts for a maximum of 72 hours. (The Code identifies the following circumstances as evidencing an emergency: an immediate and significant risk of mental or physical harm to the patient or to others; and/or the danger of serious harm to property; and/or the need for physical restraint of the patient.)[5] The applicant may be an ASW or the nearest relative. The application is founded upon one medical recommendation (which need not be from a section 12 approved doctor), with admission following within the next 24 hours. A second medical recommendation (from a

---

3   *R* v. *Wilson ex parte Williamson* [1996] COD 42.
4   This means five clear days; so if the first examination took place on 1 August the second examination must take place no later than 7 August.
5   Department of Health (1999) *Mental Health Act 1983 Code of Practice.* London: DH, paragraph 6.1. This guidance is reproduced in the 2007 Draft Code. Department of Health (2007) *Mental Health Act 1983 Draft revised Code of Practice.* London: DH, paragraph 5.7.

section 12 doctor if need be) converts the section 4 into a section 2. Part 4 of the Act (which authorises compulsory treatment) does not apply until it becomes a section 2.

Admission for treatment (section 3)

Under section 3 a patient can be admitted to hospital compulsorily and detained for treatment for an initial period of up to six months. An application for admission for treatment can be made by the nearest relative or, unless the nearest relative objects, by an ASW.

Admission must be within 14 days of the last medical examination which resulted in a recommendation. The application will be based on joint or separate written recommendations from two doctors.

The legal criteria for detention are that the patient is:

- suffering from mental illness, severe mental impairment, psychopathic disorder or mental impairment and his mental disorder is of a nature or degree which makes it appropriate for him to receive medical treatment in a hospital; and

- in the case of psychopathic disorder or mental impairment, such treatment is likely to alleviate or prevent deterioration of his condition; and

- it is necessary for the health or safety of the patient or for the protection of other persons that he should receive such treatment and it cannot be provided unless he is detained under this section.

Applications for admission for treatment may be renewed after six months, and thereafter at yearly intervals. The legal requirements justifying a renewal are discussed below.

Errors in completing forms

Mistakes will inevitably occur in completing the forms that are necessary to allow a patient to be lawfully detained under the Mental Health Act 1983.

There is commonly a failure on the part of social workers and doctors to distinguish between the relative importance of these forms and the many other forms which they are required by their employers to complete, such as those used to record after-care information.[6]

The Mental Health Act 1983 permits any application or recommendation 'which is found to be in any respect incorrect or defective'[7] to be amended by the person who completed the document provided the hospital managers agree and the amendment is made within 14 days of the patient's admission. Examples of rectifiable errors would include mis-stating names, dates and places. Errors that could not be rectified would include: failing to sign the form and medical recommendations signed after the application.

Mental Health Act 2007, section 3 amendments

The amended section will read as follows:

An application for admission for treatment may be made in respect of a patient on the grounds that:

(a)   he is suffering from mental disorder of a nature or degree which makes it appropriate for him to receive medical treatment in a hospital; and

(b)   it is necessary for the health or safety of the patient or for the protection of other persons that he should receive such treatment and it cannot be provided unless he is detained under this section; and

(c)   appropriate medical treatment is available for him.

Choice between section 2 or section 3?

The Code contains a chapter[8] detailing 'pointers' for professionals having to decide whether to use section 2 or section 3. Since section 2 is an assessment section it could be used, for example, where a patient's diagnosis is unclear or

---

6   Eldergill, E. (1997) *Mental Health Review Tribunals Law and Practice*. London: Sweet & Maxwell, page 262.

7   Mental Health Act 1983, section 15.

8   Department of Health (1999) *Mental Health Act 1983 Code of Practice*. London: DH, Chapter 5, 'Section 2 or 3?' These pointers remain largely unchanged in the 2007 Draft Code. Department of Health (2007) *Mental Health Act 1983 Draft revised Code of Practice*. London: DH, paragraph 41.1.

there has been no regular contact with mental health services. Decisions should not be influenced by the possibility that 'a patient's nearest relative objects to admission under section 3'.[9] Although mental health professionals must give consideration to Chapter 5 in the Code, they should also take into account the arguments advanced by Richard Jones that section 2 should in general be used as the initial section to detain a patient: 'The extent of any prior knowledge that might exist about the patient does not deflect from the need to assess the patient's current situation.'[10]

Leave of absence (section 17)

The use of 'section 17 leave' provides legal authority for detained patients to leave hospital for specified periods of time.

> Only the rmo can grant leave of absence to a patient formally detained under the Act. In the absence of the rmo (for example, if he or she is on annual leave or otherwise unavailable) permission can only be granted by the doctor who is for the time being in charge of the patient's treatment.[11]

The period of time for which a patient leaves hospital remains at the discretion of the RMO ('responsible clinician' when the MHA 2007 comes into force; see Chapter 4). A patient granted leave under section 17 remains 'liable to be detained' and the provisions of Part 4 of the Act continue to apply. If it becomes necessary to administer treatment in the absence of the patient's consent under Part 4, 'consideration should be given to recalling the patient to hospital'.[12]

The courts have given detailed consideration to the boundaries between 'detention' and 'liability to detention'. In the 1986 case of *Hallstrom*,[13] McCullough J held that admission under section 3 only covered those whose mental condition required a period of in-patient hospital treatment. In 1999,

---

9   Department of Health (1999) *Mental Health Act 1983 Code of Practice*. London: DH, Chapter 5, paragraph 5.3(d), page 703.

10   Jones, R. (2006) *Mental Health Act Manual*, 10th edn. London: Thomson Sweet & Maxwell, page 26, paragraph 1-033.

11   Department of Health (1999) *Mental Health Act 1983 Code of Practice*. London: DH, paragraph 20.3a.

12   Ibid., paragraph 20.8. This guidance is reproduced in the 2007 Draft Code. Department of Health (2007) *Mental Health Act 1983 Draft revised Code of Practice*. London: DH, paragraph 22.17.

13   *R v. Hallstrom ex parte W; R v. Gardner ex parte L* [1986] 2 All ER 306.

however, the court[14] concluded a renewal could take place while a patient was on section 17 leave providing the patient's care contained an element of hospital treatment. In the 2002 case of *DR*, Wilson J accepted that continuing liability to detention could only be justified 'if a significant component of the [treatment] plan is for treatment in hospital'.[15] He then abandoned any linkage between the justification for a patient's continuing liability for detention and in-patient treatment. The effect of this approach by the courts has resulted in the increased use of section 17 leave for extended periods of time.

It should be noted that there is some confusion in nomenclature at the heart of the Mental Health Act 2007. The Act refers variously to supervised community treatment (SCT) and community treatment orders (CTOs). The 2007 Draft Code refers to SCTs whereas the explanatory notes to the Act refer to CTOs. This text refers to CTOs.

Relationship between section 17 leave and community treatment orders (CTOs)

The Mental Health Act 2007 provides that longer-term leave (defined as indefinite leave or specified leave for more than seven consecutive days) may not be granted unless the responsible clinician has first considered whether a patient should go on to a CTO.

Renewal of authority to detain a patient for treatment

Authority to detain a patient under section 3 will expire after six months beginning with the date that the patient was admitted unless authority for the detention has been renewed. Conditions for renewal are set out in the Mental Health Act 1983, section 20, which also applies to guardianship orders. Section 20 requires that the RMO (responsible clinician when the Mental Health Act 2007 is in force) must examine the patient within two months of the expiry date of the section and confirm in a report that certain criteria are met, including: the nature or degree of mental disorder makes hospital treatment appropriate; detention is necessary for the health or safety of patient or protection of others; and the treatability test is met. Before completing a report the RMO must consult another professional. In the case of

---

14 *B* v. *Barking, Havering and Brentwood Community Health Care NHS Trust* [1999] 1 FLR 106.
15 *R (on the application of DR)* v. *Mersey Health Care NHS Trust* [2002] MHLR 386. See also *R (on the application of CS)* v. *MHRT* [2004] MHLR 355.

patients who are classified as being mentally ill or severely mentally impaired an alternative 'vulnerability' test is available.[16]

As the Mental Health Act 2007 introduces a new 'appropriate treatment' test and abolishes the treatability test, the renewal provisions described above will change. The consultation process will have to be evidenced in writing.[17]

Detaining patients already in hospital

Under the Mental Health Act 1983, section 5, applications for compulsory admission and detention can be made in respect of people who are informal patients. Applications for detention for treatment under section 3 can also be made for those who are already detained for assessment under section 2.

Discharging the patient

If a patient is liable to be detained under the Mental Health Act 1983, sections 2 and 3, he or she can be discharged by the RMO/responsible clinician, the nearest relative (see Chapter 4), the hospital managers and the MHRT. If a patient is liable to be detained under section 4 he or she can be discharged by the RMO/responsible clinician.

RMO (responsible clinician)

There is no formal process to be followed where a patient is discharged from section by the RMO/responsible clinician apart from the order being in writing.[18] The Guiding Principles to the Code of Practice include a statement that a patient should:

> be discharged from detention or other powers provided by the Act as soon as it is clear that their application is no longer justified.[19]

---

16   Mental Health Act 1983, section 20(4)(c), which provides that 'the patient, if discharged, is unlikely to be able to care for himself, to obtain the care which he needs or to guard himself against serious exploitation'.

17   Mental Health Act 2007, section 20, inserting 5A.

18   Mental Health Act 1983, section 23(1).

19   Department of Health (1999) *Mental Health Act 1983 Code of Practice*. London: DH, paragraph 1.1.

The Mental Health Act 2007 does not reproduce this principle. Rather guidance is provided in relation to the responsible clinician's power of discharge:

> If at any time, a responsible clinician concludes that the criteria which would justify renewing the patient's discharge or extending the patient's SCT[20] (as the case may be) are not met, the responsible clinician should exercise the power of discharge.[21]

If a patient is considered to pose a risk to the public and is found to be no longer mentally disordered, discharge from detention can be delayed for a period to allow appropriate after-care facilities to be put in place.[22] The length of time that discharge can be delayed has not yet been decided by the courts.

Hospital managers

Detained patients can request that their cases are formally reviewed by panels of managers and that they are represented at managers' hearings. Managers have a general discretion to discharge a patient:

> The essential yardstick in considering a review application is whether the grounds for admission or continued detention under the Act are satisfied.[23]

Mental Health Review Tribunals (MHRTs)

The European Court of Human Rights held in *Winterwerp* v. *Netherlands*[24] that any person (and this will include a child or young person) who has been deprived of their liberty on the grounds of unsoundness of mind should:

---

20 Supervised community treatment; also referred to as a community treatment order (CTO).
21 Department of Health (2007) *Mental Health Act 1983 Draft revised Code of Practice*. London: DH, paragraph 32.10.
22 *Johnson* v. *United Kingdom* (1999) 27 EHRR 296.
23 Department of Health (1999) *Mental Health Act 1983 Code of Practice*. London: DH, paragraph 23.11, referred to by Jackson J in *SR* v. *Huntercombe Maidenhead Hospital and others* [2005] EWHC 2361. Later in the judgment in paragraph 3.5, Jackson J observed: 'the matter which lies at the heart of this litigation is the welfare of a teenage girl [SR was 15] with serious mental health problems, who has spent almost all of the last 18 months in hospital. A huge amount of public resources has been devoted to the present litigation. I express the hope that similar resources will be devoted to her treatment in hospital and her after-care when she is fit to be released.'
24 *Winterwerp* v. *Netherlands* (1979) 2 EHRR 387, at 407–408, paragraph 60.

have access to a court and the opportunity to be heard either in person or, where necessary, through some form of representation.

In this context MHRTs are 'courts' and are designed to make patients' rights practical and effective.

Although the procedures [at MHRTs] have become more formal since the advent of legal assistance for patients, they are designed to be user-friendly and to enable the patient and her relative to communicate directly with the tribunal.[25]

This 'user-friendliness' is reflected in simple and flexible procedural rules. For example:

The tribunal may conduct the hearing in such manner as it considers most suitable bearing in mind the health and interests of the patient and it shall, so far as appears to it appropriate, seek to avoid formality in its proceedings.[26]

In recognition of the need to promote equal treatment for all involved with the MHRT a panel of tribunal members is being established to ensure that, wherever possible, a case involving a child or young person includes at least one panel member who has particular expertise in working with people from that group.

The Mental Health Act 1983, section 72, requires the MHRT to consider specific statutory criteria in deciding whether a patient should be discharged; these criteria in part mirror the wording of the criteria that must be applied where a patient is 'sectioned'. (If the MHRTs) have to consider an application by a nearest relative for the discharge of a patient, the criteria are modified to require consideration being given to whether the patient, 'if released, would be likely to act in a manner dangerous to other persons or to himself'.[27] This is because such hearings only take place where the RMO/ responsible clinician has blocked the nearest relative's exercise of their discharge powers.) MHRTs also have powers to make recommendations, for example that a patient should be transferred to another hospital.[28]

---

25   *R (on the application of H)* v. *Secretary of State for Health* [2005] 4 All ER, at 1322, paragraph 26.
26   Mental Health Review Tribunal Rules 1983, (SI 1983/942), rule 22(1).
27   Mental Health Act 1983, section 72(1)(b)(iii).
28   Ibid., section 72(3)(a).

The Code states that it is important that assistance is given to children to enable their legal representation at tribunals.[29]

APPLICATIONS AND REFERENCES TO MHRTS

Detention under many sections of the Mental Health Act 1983 gives a right to the detained person to apply to the MHRT. In addition the Act contains provisions for the managers of hospitals to refer a case to the MHRT where there has not been an application for a specific period of time. In the case of children under the age of 16 there is a specific provision: where the 'authority for the detention of patient in hospital is renewed' and one year has elapsed since the MHRT last considered the case then the hospital managers must refer the case to the MHRT.[30] This section is likely to be used rarely given that children are most unlikely to be detained for this period of time without MHRT review. More significant protection is contained in the Mental Health Act 1983, section 67, which provides for the Secretary of

---

Protecting the rights of incapable patients

Some 70 per cent of section 2 admissions do not lead to an application to a MHRT. This was referred to by Baroness Hale in the case of *R (on the application of H)* v. *Secretary of State for Health* [2005] 4 All ER 1311. One issue in this case was whether the absence of provision in the MHA to allow a patient 'incapable of exercising the right on their own initiative' was incompatible with the rights of a detained patient under Article 5(4) o f the ECHR to apply to a tribunal which can review the lawfulness of his or her detention (see Chapter 1). The House of Lords decided that the right of a patient under Article 5(4) does not require judicial authorisation in every case and that the MHA contained other safeguards. If a patient lacks capacity to apply (or in the case of a child is not competent) the Secretary of State can under section 67 of the MHA refer a patient's case to the MHRT. This happened in this case.

---

29   Department of Health (1999) *Mental Health Act 1983 Code of Practice*. London: DH, paragraph 31.20. The 2007 Draft Code advises that 'Hospital managers should actively promote that an application is made to the MHRT by the child or young person, particularly following their initial detention.' Department of Health (2007) *Mental Health Act 1983 Draft revised Code of Practice*. London: DH, paragraph 39.52.
30   Mental Health Act 1983, section 68(2). This is now extended to any person under the age of 18 by the Mental Health Act 2007, section 68(6).

State at any time to refer to a MHRT the case of any patient detained under Part 2 of the Act. (Part 2 deals with the processes of civil detention, Part 3 deals with mentally disordered offenders.)

Planning for discharge

It must be in the interests of every child or young person whose case is to be reviewed by a MHRT (or the hospital managers) for the professionals involved in the case to make sure that the best evidence available is prepared and made available to the reviewing body. The Code states that:

> some discussion of after-care needs, including social services and other relevant professionals and agencies, should take place before a patient has a Mental Health Review Tribunal or managers' hearing, so that suitable after-care arrangements can be implemented in the event of his or her being discharged.[31]

In all cases involving children and young people there should be much more than a discussion prior to the hearing. The MHRT rules require that the 're-sponsible authority' make available to the MHRT certain reports. The 're-sponsible authority' is defined in the MHRT Rules[32] as being the managers of the hospital in which the patient is liable to be detained; this includes both NHS and private hospitals. The Rules also specify what information should be contained in reports.[33] For example, a social circumstance report must contain the following information:

1. the patient's home and family circumstances, including the attitude of the patient's nearest relative or the person so acting

2. the opportunities for employment or occupation and the housing facilities which would be available to the patient if discharged

3. the availability of community support and relevant medical facilities

4. the financial circumstances of the patient.

---

31   Department of Health (1999) *Mental Health Act 1983 Code of Practice.* London: DH, paragraph 27.7. (This guidance is not reproduced in the 2007 Draft Code.)
32   Mental Health Review Tribunal Rules 1983 (SI 1983/942), rule 2.
33   Ibid., schedule 1, Part B.

The tribunal, like any court, can issue directions for information to be made available. If the responsible authority is not able to provide the necessary information because, for example, the statutory authorities responsible for the child's after-care have not been able to make decisions about funding a particular placement, then the making of directions should be considered. For these to be effective they must be precise, and directed at the right organisation, and the person within that organisation must have the requisite level of seniority. For example, decisions about funding a particular placement are likely to be made within a joint commissioning framework established by health and children's services and any directions that are made should reflect this.

At a minimum, the tribunal should always have available a comprehensive care plan detailing the arrangements that need to be in place if the child were to be discharged. It is suggested that the guidance contained in Local Authority Circular (99)29 on the appropriate contents of a care plan within care proceedings (reproduced in Appendix 2) should be used to structure any care plan. The contents can be modified to take into account the particular circumstances of the case, for example agreements as to funding any proposed placement and confirmation of the funding of those arrangements.

2 – Other orders

Emergency orders
SECTION 135

Section 135(1) allows a magistrates court to issue a warrant on the application of an ASW to allow a police officer to enter premises, if need be by force, and, if thought fit, remove a person believed to be suffering from a mental disorder to a place of safety with a view to making an application under the Mental Health Act 1983 or 'other arrangements for his treatment or care'.[34] The police officer must be accompanied by an ASW and doctor. The maximum period of detention under the section is 72 hours from the moment of arrival at the place of safety.

Section 135(2) covers the issue of a warrant to enter premises and remove patients who are already liable to be detained or subject to guardianship. This section would, for example, cover patients who have gone absent without leave.

---

34   Mental Health Act 1983, section 135(1)(b).

SECTION 136

This section provides authority for a police officer to remove to a 'place of safety'[35] a person found in a place to which the public have access, if the person appears to be suffering from mental disorder and to be in immediate need of care or control and the officer thinks it is necessary in the interests of the person or for the protection of others. The duration of the authority to detain is 72 hours from the moment of arrival at the place of safety.

The purpose of the section is to allow a patient to be safely assessed by an ASW and a doctor. If after the doctor has examined the person subject to section 136 and concludes:

> that he or she is not mentally disordered within the meaning of the Act then the individual can no longer be detained under the section and should be immediately discharged from detention.[36]

Where a person is in police detention under section 136 their removal is deemed to be an arrest and so they have rights under PACE[37] including a right of access to legal advice.

Under section 136 it is not lawful to convey a person from one place of safety to another. The Mental Health Act 2007 amends this provision to allow the police or an AMHP to authorise movement between places of safety. This will be helpful if, for example, the person needs to go to the accident and emergency department of a hospital. (This amendment will also cover patients on a section 135.)

Community orders

GUARDIANSHIP AND SUPERVISED AFTER-CARE

Guardianship[38] and supervised after-care[39] are only available if the patient is aged 16 or over. The purpose of guardianship, according to the Code, is to

---

35   Place of safety is defined as 'residential accommodation provided by a local social services authority under Part III of the NAA [National Assistance Act] 1948, a hospital as defined by this Act, a police station, an independent hospital or care home for mentally disordered persons or any other suitable place the occupier of which is willing temporarily to receive the patient'. Mental Health Act 1983, section 135(6).

36   Department of Health (1999) *Mental Health Act 1983 Code of Practice*. London: DH, paragraph 10.8(a).

37   Police and Criminal Evidence Act 1984, sections 56 and 58, and PACE Detention Code C.

38   Mental Health Act 1983, section 7.

39   Ibid., section 25A–J.

enable patients to receive community care where it cannot be provided without the use of compulsory powers.[40]

The Mental Health (Patients in the Community) Act 1995 amended the Mental Health Act 1983 by introducing the power to direct after-care under supervision. (All the provisions relating to supervised aftercare will be repealed by the MHA 2007.)

These orders give authority to social service or health professionals, respectively, to require patients to: reside at a specified place; attend at places and at times so specified for the purpose of medical treatment, occupation, education or training; and give access to the patient at any time, at any place where the patient is residing, to any doctor, ASW or other person so specified.

These powers are not 'community treatment orders' in that a patient subject to guardianship or supervised after-care cannot be compulsorily treated without their consent outside hospital. The guardian has no power to 'take and convey' the patient to any of the places the patient is required to be for medical treatment, occupation, education and training.[41] However, if the patient is absent, without leave, from the place in which he or she resides, the patient may be taken into custody and returned to that place.[42] If a patient is placed on supervised after-care the supervisor has the power to take and convey the patient to:

> any place where the patient is required to reside or to attend for the purpose of medical treatment, occupation, education or training.[43]

Supervised after-care can be ended by the CRMO (Community Responsible Medical Officer) or the MHRT. Guardianship can be discharged by the RMO/responsible clinician, the local authority, the nearest relative or the MHRT.

COMMUNITY TREATMENT ORDERS

The MHA 2007 abolishes supervised after-care (section 25A) and replaces it with community treatment orders (CTOs). Confusingly CTOs are also

---

40   Department of Health (1999) *Mental Health Act 1983 Code of Practice*. London: DH, paragraph 13.1.

41   The MHA 2007 schedule 3 paragraph 3(5) amends the MHA by introducing a new power to take and convey a person to their required place of residence.

42   Mental Health Act 1983, section 18(3).

43   Ibid., section 25D(4).

referred to in the Act, and the 2007 Code, as supervised community treatment provisions (SCTs).

Overview of CTOs

Chapter 4 (sections 32–36) of the MHA 2007 sets out the general regime for CTOs. These include the criteria for making a CTO, the conditions that can be applied to a person subject to a CTO, the duration of the CTO, the power to recall a person subject to a CTO to hospital and the authority to treat individuals who are subject to a CTO and who have not been recalled to hospital. There is no age restriction on CTOs.

> The supervised community treatment (SCT) provisions will allow some patients with a mental disorder to live in the community whilst still being subject to powers under the 1983 Act. Only those patients who are detained in hospital for treatment will be eligible to be considered for SCT... Patients on SCT may be recalled to hospital for treatment should this become necessary.[44]

Although the patient's nearest relative does not have to be consulted before a CTO is made, the nearest relative may apply to discharge a CTO; this maybe blocked by the responsible clinician if the statutory grounds are met. A patient may apply to a MHRT for the order to be discharged and the hospital managers may also discharge a CTO. There is an automatic reference procedure to allow the MHRT to review CTO cases where there has not been an application for a specific period of time or where the order has been revoked.

Scope of the CTO treatment provisions

Section 35 ('Authority to treat') introduces a range of consent to treatment provisions which will apply to those individuals who are subject to CTOs and have not been recalled to hospital. They cover 'adult community patients' (those aged 16 years and over) and 'child community patients' (those aged under 16 years). The provisions apply to 'relevant treatment' which includes medication for mental disorder. The Act provides that relevant treatment cannot be given to a community patient unless there is

---

44   Department of Health (2007) *Mental Health Act 2007 Explanatory Notes*. London: DH, paragraph 107.

authority to give the treatment. For certain types of treatment it will also be necessary for 'certificate requirement' to be met.[45]

Individuals subject to CTOs who have capacity (or, in the case of child community patients, 'competence') to make treatment decisions *can only* be treated in the community if they *consent* to such treatment. If they refuse treatment this is likely to lead to their recall to hospital, where they can be treated without their consent.

The Act authorises the treatment of a person subject to a CTO, who is under 18 and lacks capacity/competence, without their being recalled to hospital in two circumstances:

- *Non-emergency treatment.* 16–18-year-olds and child community patients can be given non-emergency treatment without consent if they lack capacity/competence and specified conditions are met.

- *Emergency treatment.* 16–18-year-olds or child community patients who lack capacity/competence can be given emergency treatment, and in such cases the Act provides that force can be used where it is a proportionate response to prevent harm to the patient.

CTOs and children

When assessing whether a child or young person may be suitable for a CTO, the 2007 Draft Code advises:

Where the patient is under the age of 18 the responsible clinician and the AMHP should bear in mind that the most age-appropriate treatment may be that provided by a Child and Adolescent Mental Health Service (CAMHS).[46]

The following guidance is also contained in relation to the role of the parents of a patient on a CTO (referred to in the passage as SCT):

---

45   Mental Health Act 2007, section 64B (patients 16 or over) and 64E (child community patients). A second opinion appointed doctor (SOAD) must certify in writing that the treatment may be given. This is not required for emergency treatment. Nor does it apply to the administration of medication for mental disorder for an initial period of 'one month from when a patient leaves hospital or three months from when the medication was first given to the patient (whether that medication was given in the community or in hospital) whichever is later'. Department of Health (2007) *Mental Health Act 2007 Explanatory Notes.* London: DH, paragraph 133.

46   Department of Health (2007) *Mental Health Act 1983 Draft revised Code of Practice.* London: DH, paragraph 28.6.

Parents (or other people with parental responsibility) may not consent on a child's behalf to treatment for mental disorder (or refuse it) while the child is an SCT patient any more than they can whilst the child is being detained in hospital under the Act. However, if SCT patients under the age of 18 are living with one or both of their parents, the person giving the treatment should consult with the parent(s) about the particular treatment (subject to any outweighing considerations of confidentiality). This dialogue should continue throughout the patient's treatment on SCT. If a parent is unhappy with the particular treatment, and the child is not competent to consent, a review by the patient's team should take place to consider whether the treatment and care plan, and SCT in general, is still appropriate for the child.[47]

Conditions

The only conditions that must be applied relate to the patient making himself available for examination: by the responsible clinician prior to assessment for extension of an order renewal and by a SOAD in relation to certification under Part 4A of the Act. Otherwise it will for the responsible clinician and the AMHP to set conditions providing they fall within the purpose of the Act. The 2007 Code advises that such conditions:

> might cover the arrangements for treatment in the community, and where the patient is to live. For some patients, they might cover matters such as the avoidance of illegal drugs, if that is a known risk factor. It might be appropriate to require a patient to try to avoid certain high risk situations known to place them at high risk of harm.[48]

Conclusions

The MHA is not 'a child-centred jurisdiction'.[49] Whilst this is undoubtedly correct one function of the Act is to protect a patient's rights, for example by making available independent scrutiny in relation to treatment decisions under section 58 and allowing independent representation at Mental Health Review Tribunals. Also, the amendments to the MHA made by the 2007 Act, and the guidance in the new Code, reflect a growing awareness of the need

---

47   Ibid., paragraph 25.59.
48   Ibid., paragraph 28.19.
49   Re F (Mental Health Act: Guardianship) [2000] 1 FLR 192 at 199G.

to accommodate the interests of children and young people where the use of the Act is being considered. If the MHA is going to be used to detain and treat children and young people without their consent, and the numbers may increase with the change to the Act, then the processes of assessment, detention, treatment and discharge need to be fully understood.

Attention to detail in the management of a case concerning a young person or child with complex mental health problems is essential. This should happen at all stages in the process of assessment, admission, treatment and discharge. In particular, no child should be discharged without proper arrangements being in place for their after-care.

Case examples

A psychiatrist with section 12 approval, an ASW and a GP are asked to attend the home of G, a young man aged 17, in order to interview him. His mother has become extremely concerned about his mental health, and has asked the community mental health team to assess whether he requires admission to psychiatric hospital.

G is known to CAMHS and has been treated for bipolar disorder. He was admitted to hospital last year on a section. His compliance with after-care has been erratic, and for the last six months he has refused all contact with services apart from his GP, who he saw once. Unlike the previous occasion when he was admitted for manic episodes, he now appears to be depressed and expresses delusions of a nihilistic nature. He claims to be Satan and to be responsible for all the evil in the world.

G lives on his own and his accommodation appears to be in a chaotic and unhygienic state. He is a registered student at the nearby further education college but has not participated in his course for some weeks. He appears to have lost a considerable amount of weight. He does not recognise his GP and, when it is suggested that he comes to hospital, appears not to understand. The ASW speaks to his mother who lives nearby and has a close relationship with G. She says that her son needs to go to hospital but does not need to be sectioned; she also feels that the medication which he received in the past was of little benefit.

How should the assessment be conducted? Is informal or compulsory admission appropriate? If compulsory admission is necessary, which section would be appropriate?

AA is aged 17. She was diagnosed as suffering from a bipolar disorder when she was aged 15. She has been admitted to psychiatric hospital on at least three occasions over the last two years, always under section. When she becomes unwell she is not compliant with treatment, particularly medication. Her mental health then rapidly deteriorates and she becomes aggressive and sexually disinhibited and is at high risk of being harmed by others. When unwell she also cannot care for herself. To avoid relapse the clinical team regards it as essential for AA to receive medication. She responds rapidly to medication but finds it difficult to remain compliant with it because she does not like the side effects.

She was last admitted to hospital four months ago on section 3. She was treated as an in-patient in an acute psychiatric ward for two months. She was then given section 17 leave with conditions that she reside in a hostel and return to the ward every two weeks to be given depot medication. She trusts the in-patient nurses and although she is reluctant to take medication she has remained compliant. She is, however, very clear that she would not take medication if 'she did not have to' and would not agree to receive medication from a community psychiatric nurse (CPN) who could come to the hostel.

Identify the statutory frameworks that could be used to manage her case in the community.

Chapter 6

Criminal Justice

Introduction

This book does not cover the law in relation to children and young people who are involved with the criminal justice system in any detail. Out of recognition, however, that some young people will move between the criminal justice system and in-patient psychiatric care the provisions in relation to mentally disordered offenders are outlined.

One particular area of interface is the secure accommodation regime. Secure accommodation orders may be made by the courts in criminal proceedings and in family proceedings. (The criteria justifying the orders being made vary according to the nature of the proceedings.) Chapter 3 deals with secure accommodation.

By way of background, young offenders are at high risk of suffering mental health problems; 40 per cent have a diagnosable disorder. Many of these children suffer from conduct disorders. Out of the total caseload of CAMHS, 5 per cent were young offenders.[1]

Age of criminal responsibility

The Children and Young Persons Act 1933[2] provides that:

> It is conclusively presumed that persons under the age of 10 cannot be guilty of any offence.

---

1   British Medical Association (2006) *Child and Adolescent Mental Health: A Guide for Healthcare Professionals*, www.bma.org.uk (accessed 18.12.07).
2   Children and Young Persons Act 1933, section 50.

The common law presumed that children between 10 and 14 were incapable of committing crime. This presumption was abolished by the Crime and Disorder Act 1998 for any offence committed on or after 30 September 1998. This may, as Ashford, Chard and Redhouse (2006) comment, produce very harsh results: 'The criminal law makes few concessions to the youth of the accused.'[3]

Community orders

The criminal courts may consider the following disposals where the mental health of a child or young person justifies the orders being made.

Supervision order

'The supervision order is the most flexible youth court sentence.'[4] It has no minimum age limit; it may be imposed upon any offender under 18. The maximum duration of the order is three years. Requirements can be attached including a requirement that the offender receive treatment for mental disorder.[5] This requirement can include treatment as a resident patient in a private or NHS psychiatric hospital (not a Special Hospital) and a care home.[6]

Community rehabilitation order

This order (still referred to by most as a probation order) may only be imposed on an offender who is aged 16 or over. The maximum duration of the order is three years. As with a supervision order, requirements can be attached, including a requirement that the offender receive treatment for mental disorder and a requirement as to residence.

---

3   Ashford, M., Chard, A. and Redhouse, N. (2006) *Defending Young People in the Criminal Justice System*, 3rd edn. London: Legal Action Group, page 119, paragraph 6.13.
4   Ibid., page 508, paragraph 23.127.
5   Powers of Criminal Court (Sentencing) Act 2000, Schedule 6.
6   A care home is defined in the Care Standards Act 2000 (section 3) as including accommodation together with nursing or personal care for any of the following persons who are or have been: ill, mentally disordered, disabled or infirm and/or dependent on alcohol or drugs.

Medical evidence for supervision and community rehabilitation orders

The court must be satisfied on the basis of evidence from a section 12 approved doctor that the mental condition of the offender is such as requires and may be susceptible to treatment, but is not such as to warrant the making of a hospital or guardianship order.[7]

Guardianship

The MHA provides for a person over the age of 16[8] convicted of an offence to be placed under guardianship. (See Chapter 5 for the conditions that can be attached to a guardianship order.)

Detention in hospital

Detention under the Mental Health Act 1983 for assessment followed by treatment can be effected by using the powers of civil detention, section 2 or 3; or Part 3 of the Mental Health Act which relates to the assessment and treatment of mentally disordered offenders. A Part 3 patient who has been conditionally discharged may be subject to the compulsory powers contained in Part 2 of the Mental Health Act.[9] All the orders referred to in the sections below require medical evidence from at least one section 12 approved doctor.[10] Where a section 41 restriction order or a section 45A limitation direction is being considered one doctor must attend court to give evidence.[11]

Detaining the offender patient prior to sentence

The Mental Health Act 1983 orders that are likely to be used in the criminal courts relating to children and young people are as follows.

---

7   For supervision orders, Powers of Criminal Court (Sentencing) Act 2000, Schedule 6, paragraph 6(1); for community rehabilitation orders, Powers of Criminal Court (Sentencing) Act 2000, Schedule 2, paragraph 5(1).
8   Mental Health Act 1983, section 37(2)(a)(ii).
9   *R* v. *North West London Mental Health NHS Trust ex parte Stewart* [1997] 4 All ER 871.
10 Mental Health Act 1983, section 54.
11 Ibid., section 41(2).

Section 35

This allows a crown court or a youth court to remand an accused person to a hospital for a report on his mental condition. The power can only be used if it would be impracticable for a report on his or her mental condition to be made if he or she were remanded on bail and Part 4 of the Act does not apply. Therefore, medical treatment for mental disorder cannot be given to the child or young person without his or her consent.

Section 36

This allows the remand of an accused person to hospital for treatment. This power is only available in the crown court.

Mental Health Act 2007, section 31 amendments

Section 31 of the Mental Health Act 2007 amends section 39 of the 1983 Act (information as to hospitals) to provide that a court may request information from a primary care trust (PCT) (in England) or local health board (LHB) (in Wales) when dealing with a person aged under 18 in certain cases. Those cases are where the court is considering making a hospital order or interim hospital order, to remand the person to hospital for a report on their mental condition (section 35) or for treatment (section 36), or (in the case of a magistrates' court) to order detention in hospital when committing an offender to the crown court (section 44). The information will be about the availability of accommodation or facilities designed to be specially suitable for patients under 18. The purpose of this provision is to ensure that courts do not place a child in a prison setting when a suitable hospital bed would be a more appropriate option.

Section 31 also amends section 140 of the 1983 Act (notification of hospitals having arrangements for reception of urgent cases) to place a duty on PCTs and LHBs to advise local social service authorities in their area of hospitals providing accommodation specially suitable for patients aged under 18.

This section is unlikely to be operational until April 2010 at the earliest.

Sentencing the mentally disordered offender under the Mental Health Act

Section 37 (hospital order)

The grounds for making a section 37 hospital order are that either the youth court or the crown court are satisfied on the basis of written or oral evidence from two doctors that the offender is suffering from mental illness, psychopathic disorder, severe mental impairment or mental impairment and that either:

- the mental disorder from which the offender is suffering is of a nature or degree which makes it appropriate for him to be detained in a hospital for medical treatment and, in the case of psychopathic disorder or mental impairment, that such treatment is likely to alleviate or prevent a deterioration of his/her condition; or

- in the case of an offender who has attained the age of 16 years, the mental disorder is of a nature or degree which warrants his reception into guardianship under this Act; and

- the court is of the opinion, having regard to all circumstances including the nature of the offence and the character and antecedents of the offender, and to the other available methods of dealing with him, that the most suitable method of disposing of the case is by means of an order under this section.

The legal status of a patient detained under section 37 does not differ significantly from a patient detained under section 3 except the patient's nearest relative has a right to apply to a MHRT during the second six months of the patient's detention and then at yearly intervals.[12] The patient can only make his or her first application during the second six months.

Section 41 (restriction order)

Where a person over the age of 14 is found guilty of an imprisonable offence and the grounds for making a hospital order are satisfied, the crown court can attach a restriction order to a section 37 order. The youth court or magistrates court may commit the defendant to the crown court with a view to a restriction order being made, but only if the offender is over the age of 14

---

12   Ibid., section 69(1)(a).

and has been found guilty of an imprisonable offence. The committal shall be in custody.

The grounds for making a restriction order are that the court decides that, having regard to the nature of the offence, the antecedents of the offender and the risk of him or her committing further offences if set at large, it is necessary for the protection of the public from serious harm to make a restriction order.[13]

The effect of a restriction order is that decisions about the offender's leave of absence, transfer and discharge will be taken by the Secretary of State. A decision to discharge a restriction order patient can be made either by the Secretary of State or the Mental Health Review Tribunal.

Restriction orders can now only be made without limit of time.

Restricted patients do not have a nearest relative. This is because they have no function under the MHA.[14] Where a social circumstance report is prepared in relation to a patient subject to a restriction order the details of the patient's relative should be omitted.

Section 38 (interim hospital order)

Where a person is convicted by the crown court or magistrates court and he or she is suffering from one of the four specific categories of mental disorder, then the court may make a hospital order authorising his or her admission to hospital for a finite period of time (up to 12 months).[15] The purpose of this order is to allow an evaluation to be made of the mentally disordered offender's response to detention which will allow the treatment providers to establish the appropriateness of making a full hospital order on the expiry of the section 38 order.

Section 45A (limitation direction)

When a crown court imposes a prison sentence on an offender for particular categories of very serious offences, where the sentence is 'not fixed by law'[16] and the offender is classified as suffering from psychopathic disorder, the

---

13   Ibid., section 41(1).
14   *R (on the application of H)* v. *MHRT* [2000] MHLR 203.
15   Mental Health Act 1983, section 38, as amended by Crime Sentences Act 1997, section 49(1).
16   Mental Health Act 1983, section 45A(1).

court can direct immediate admission to psychiatric hospital. The changes to the definition of mental disorder by the MHA 2007, and in particular the abolition of the term 'psychopathic disorder', may mean that this section will be used more frequently.

Transfers from the 'juvenile secure estate' to psychiatric hospitals

This phrase is used here to provide a collective description of the types of institutions where a child or young person convicted of a criminal offence may serve his or her sentence.[17] 'The Youth Justice Board considers that there are up to 300 young people in secure establishments requiring transfer to specialist mental health facilities at any one time.'[18]

The MHA contains detailed provisions for the transfer of prisoners serving sentences of imprisonment, from prisons, or in the context of this book from the juvenile secure estate, to psychiatric hospitals.

Section 47 (transfer direction)

The Mental Health Act states:

> In the case of a person serving a sentence of imprisonment, if the Secretary of State is satisfied, by reports from at least two registered medical practitioners:
>
> - that the said person is suffering from mental illness, psychopathic disorder, severe mental impairment or mental impairment; and
>
> - that the mental disorder from which that person is suffering is of a nature or degree which makes it appropriate for him to be detained in a hospital for medical treatment and, in the case of psychopathic

---

17   'Working Together' under the heading 'The Secure Estate for children and young people' describes the statutory responsibility of the Youth Justice Board for England and Wales (YJB) which is for the commissioning and purchasing of all secure accommodation for children and for setting standards for the delivery of those services. The Secure Estate comprises Prison Service accommodation for juveniles (juvenile Young Offenders' Institutions), Secure Training Centres and Secure Children's Homes provided by local authorities. *Working Together to Safeguard Children: A Guide to Inter-agency Working to Safeguard and Promote the Welfare of Children* (2006). London: TSO, paragraph 2.112.

18   Ashford, M., Chard, A. and Redhouse, N. (2006) *Defending Young People in the Criminal Justice System*, 3rd edn. London: Legal Action Group, page 693, paragraph 30.25, referencing *Youth Justice 2004: Bringing Young People to Justice* (2004). London: Audit Commission.

disorder or mental impairment, that such treatment is likely to alleviate or prevent a deterioration of his condition;

the Secretary of State may, if he is of the opinion having regard to the public interest and all the circumstances that it is expedient so to do, by warrant direct that person be removed to and detained in such hospital as may be specified in the direction; and a direction under this section shall be known as 'a transfer direction'.

Section 49 (restriction direction)

The Secretary of State can impose a restriction direction at the same time as making the transfer direction. The effect of this is that for the duration of the person's sentence the person will be treated as if he or she is subject to a restriction order.

Mental Health Review Tribunals

Patients detained under nearly all the sections referred to above have a right to have their cases periodically reviewed by Mental Health Review Tribunals. The powers of the tribunals will vary according to the section of the Mental Health Act 1983 under which the patient is detained.

Unfitness to plead

The Criminal Procedure (Insanity) Act 1964 makes provision for persons found to be not guilty by reason of insanity or to be unfit to plead in respect of criminal charges. If the court determines the defendant to have done the act or made the omission charged against him or her then the following disposals are available: a hospital order (with or without restrictions), a supervision order or an absolute discharge. A hospital order can only be made if the conditions contained in section 37 (see above) are met.

Chapter 7
The Mental Capacity Act 2005

Introduction

The Mental Capacity Act 2005 (MCA) became fully operational on 1 October 2007. The Act establishes a comprehensive framework for decision making for persons aged 16 or over who may lack capacity to make specific decisions for themselves. It is important to stress that capacity is decision specific; for example, a person may have capacity to make a decision in relation to a straightforward dental procedure but may lack capacity to make a decision in relation to a more complicated medical procedure. According to the Mental Capacity Act Code of Practice, the Act is intended to 'assist and support people who may lack capacity'.[1]

Chapter 12 of the Mental Capacity Act Code of Practice, 'How does the Act apply to children and young people?', is reproduced in Appendix 4.

General principles

The MCA contains a number of general principles. These principles are as follows:

1. A person must be assumed to have capacity unless it is established that he lacks capacity.

2. A person is not to be treated as unable to make a decision unless all practicable steps to help him to do so have been taken without success.

---

1   Department of Constitutional Affairs (2007) *Mental Capacity Act 2005 Code of Practice.* London: TSO, paragraph 1.4.

3.   A person is not to be treated as unable to make a decision merely because he makes an unwise decision.

4.   An act done, or decision made, under the Mental Capacity Act 2005 for or on behalf of a person who lacks capacity must be done, or made, in his best interests.

5.   Before the act is done, or the decision is made, regard must be had to whether the purpose for which it is needed can be as effectively achieved in a way that is less restrictive of the person's rights and freedom of action.

Identifying and determining incapacity

The Mental Capacity Act 2005 defines a person who lacks capacity as follows:

> A person lacks capacity in relation to a matter if at the material time he is unable to make a decision for himself in relation to the matter because of an impairment of, or a disturbance in the functioning of, the mind or brain.[2]

This means that two questions always need to be asked to identify incapacity:

1.   Is there an impairment of, or disturbance in, the functioning of the person's mind or brain?

2.   Is that impairment or disturbance sufficient to make the person unable to make the decision in question?

The Mental Capacity Act Code of Practice identifies the situation where a 16- to 17-year-old may be unable to make a decision for reasons other than having an impairment or disturbance in the functioning of mind or brain, for example because the young person is 'overwhelmed by the implications of the decision'.[3] If that were to be the case then the Mental Capacity Act 2005 would not have any application. This is an issue which requires consideration. If an adult were overwhelmed by the implications of a particular decision rendering them incapable of making that decision, it is likely that

---

2   Mental Capacity Act 2005, section 2(1).
3   Department of Constitutional Affairs (2007) *Mental Capacity Act 2005 Code of Practice.* London: TSO, paragraph 12.13.

he or she would be regarded as lacking capacity to make the decision in question; the person has a (perhaps temporary) impairment or disturbance of the working of their mind or brain.[4] It is not immediately apparent why a 16- to 17-year-old unable to make the same decision should be treated any differently. It could however be argued that the young person's incapacity is related to their particular stage of development rather than any other factors.

The Mental Capacity Act 2005 is situation specific. For example, does the person have capacity to make a decision about a particular form of medical treatment at the time that the decision needs to be made? Does the lack of capacity relate to the particular decision in question? This approach to defining a person as incapacitated only in relation to a particular decision at a particular time has been described as the functional approach. This approach should be contrasted with the application of the Mental Health Act 1983 to decision making.

If a person suffers from a mental disorder within the meaning of the Mental Health Act 1983, and is then detained under that Act, then any, or all, of the decisions that person may make about their medical treatment for mental disorder are subject to statutory control. In particular, if a treatment falls within section 63 of the Act then a decision to refuse treatment can be overridden, despite the fact that the patient may have capacity in relation to the decision in question. Safeguards in relation to certain treatments provided under sections 58 and 59 of the Act (for example the provision of ECT) may require certification as to the capacity of the patient by a second opinion approved doctor (SOAD). For detailed discussion of this area see Chapter 4.

The Mental Capacity Act 2005 sets out tests for determining whether a person is unable to make a decision:

A person is unable to make a decision for himself if he is unable:

(a) to understand the information relevant to the decision,

(b) to retain that information,

(c) to use or weigh that information as part of the process of making the decision, or

(d) to communicate his decision (whether by talking, using sign language or any other means).[5]

---

4   *Re MB (Medical Treatment)* [1997] 2 FLR 426.
5   Mental Capacity Act 2005, section 3(1).

Protection from liability

The Mental Capacity Act 2005 section 5 allows both professionals and carers to take actions in connection with the care or treatment of a person lacking capacity to consent to a particular action without the need to obtain any formal authority. These actions could involve the use of restraint. This provides protection to professionals and carers against civil liability for actions done under the Mental Capacity Act 2005, so long as those actions are carried out in accordance with the Act's principles, and in particular are in the best interests of the person lacking capacity to consent to them. The protection provided by this section is not unlimited and so liability for negligence is unaffected.[67]

The appropriate use of restraint

The Mental Capacity Act 2005 Code of Practice contains the following scenario to illustrate the 'appropriate use of restraint'.

Derek, a man with learning disabilities, has begun to behave in a challenging way. Staff at his care home think he might have a medical condition that is causing him distress. They take him to the doctor, who thinks that Derek might have a hormone imbalance. But the doctor needs to take a blood test to confirm this, and when he tries to take the test Derek attempts to fight him off.

The results might be negative – so the test might not be necessary. But the doctor decides that a test is in Derek's best interests, because failing to treat a problem like a hormone imbalance might make it worse. It is therefore in Derek's best interests to restrain him to take the blood test. The temporary restraint is in proportion to the likely harm caused by failing to treat a possible medical condition.[7]

---

6 Ibid., section 5(3).
7 Department of Constitutional Affairs (2007) *Mental Capacity Act 2005 Code of Practice*. London: TSO, page 107.

Restraint or deprivation of liberty?

Restraint which is permissible within section 5 is qualified by section 6 of the Mental Capacity Act 2005. First, the restraint used must be 'proportionate'. Second, section 5 will afford no protection if the restraint used amounts to a deprivation of liberty within Article 5 of the European Convention on Human Rights (ECHR).[8]

To avoid the consequences of an unlawful deprivation of liberty the government has enacted a statutory framework for the protection of adults. The Mental Health Act 2007 has been used to amend the Mental Capacity Act 2005 to introduce a raft of safeguards known as the 'Bournewood safeguards'.[9] (These are not likely to become operational until April 2009 at the earliest.) Section 25 of the Children Act provides children and young people with statutory protection and so they are expressly excluded from the Bournewood safeguards.[10]

Although what amounts to a deprivation of liberty is discussed elsewhere in this book the limits imposed by the application of section 6 in relation to young people can be illustrated by way of an example:[11]

> A 17-year-old is assessed as not having the capacity to make a decision about a proposed intervention. The Mental Capacity Act could be used to authorise treatment if the conditions for its use are met. But if the primary purpose of the intervention is not to provide medical treatment for the mental disorder but to detain the child, consideration should be given to using section 25 of the Children Act.

---

8   Mental Capacity Act 2005, section 6(5).
9   The term refers to the Bournewood case discussed in Chapter 1. 'On 5 October 2004, the European Court of Human Rights (ECtHR) gave judgment in the case of *HL* v. *the United Kingdom* (commonly referred to as the "Bournewood" judgment). The ECtHR held that HL, an autistic man who lacked the capacity to consent to, or to refuse, admission to hospital for treatment, was deprived of his liberty when he was admitted informally to Bournewood Hospital.' Department of Health (2006) *The Bournewood Safeguards: Draft Illustrative Guidance.* London: DH, paragraph 1.
10   The Mental Health Act 2007 inserts schedules into the Mental Capacity Act 2005 which contain the 'Bournewood safeguards'. 'The relevant person [to qualify for safeguards] meets the age requirement if he has reached 18.' Mental Health Act 2007, Schedule 7, Schedule A1, Part 3, section 13.
11   This example is an amended version of a case example contained in the 2007 Draft Code. Department of Health (2007) *Mental Health Act 1983 Draft revised Code of Practice.* London: DH, Example E, pages 226–227.

Best interests

The Mental Capacity Act 2005 does not define 'best interests' but instead sets out a 'checklist' of factors which must be taken into account when determining someone's best interests.[12] It is important not to make assumptions about someone's best interests merely on the basis of their age or appearance, condition or any aspect of their behaviour. All relevant circumstances relating to the decision in question must be considered, including:

- whether the person may regain capacity to make the decision, and if so, when

- the need to involve the person as fully as possible

- taking account of the person's past and present wishes and feelings (in particular if they have been written down), their beliefs and values and any other factors that may have influenced them

- consulting with other people where appropriate, including anyone previously named by the person as someone to be consulted, carers or other people interested in the person's welfare, and any attorney or deputy appointed for the person (see below)

- whether there are other options which are less restrictive of the person's rights or freedom of action

- if the decision relates to life-sustaining treatment, the decision-maker must not be motivated by a desire to bring about the person's death.

All of the factors which are relevant to the particular circumstances of a case must be considered and weighed up in order to work out what decision or course of action is in the person's best interests.

Other provisions in the Act

Provisions are also made in the Mental Capacity Act 2005 to enable people to plan ahead for a future time when they may lose capacity, by creating a 'lasting power of attorney' (LPA). LPAs replace enduring powers of attorney (EPAs), and extend the scheme of substitute decision making to cover personal welfare (including healthcare) decisions as well as financial affairs,

---

12   Mental Capacity Act 2005, section 4.

if that is the donor's choice. An LPA may only be made by persons who are 18 or over.

The Mental Capacity Act 2005 also clarifies the law in relation to advance decisions to refuse medical treatment (again only applying to persons who have reached 18) and contains provisions regulating research in relation to persons who lack capacity to consent to their participation in research projects.

A new specialist court, the Court of Protection, is established with wide-ranging powers to resolve disputes and make decisions affecting people who lack capacity to make those decisions for themselves or, in some cases, to appoint another person (called a deputy) to make such decisions on behalf of the person lacking capacity.

The local authority or health authority must consult an independent mental capacity advocate (IMCA) where a decision is to be made about either serious medical treatment or the provision of, or a change of, long-term accommodation. The authorities have a discretion to consult in other circumstances, including accommodation reviews.

These provisions will only apply where the young person is adjudged to lack capacity in relation to the decision in question and there are no 'appropriate' family or friends to represent and support them.[13] In an emergency, decisions can be made on behalf of the incapacitated person without an advocate being appointed.[14]

The Mental Capacity Act 2005 and children under 16

The Mental Capacity Act 2005 has limited direct application to children under 16, since decisions concerning the care and welfare of children are already governed by the Children Act 1989. Some provision, however, is made in the Act for decision making in relation to the property of children whose disabilities are likely to cause a lack of capacity to continue into adulthood.

---

13   'If a family disagrees with a decision-maker's proposed action, this is not grounds for concluding that there is nobody whose views are relevant to the decision.' Department of Constitutional Affairs (2007) Mental Capacity Act 2005 Code of Practice, London: TSO, page 210 paragraph 10.79.

14   Ibid., section 35, and Mental Capacity Act 2005 (Independent Mental Capacity Advocates) (Expansion of Role) Regulations 2006.

The powers of the Court of Protection are extended to make decisions (including the appointment of a deputy) relating to the property and affairs of a person under 16 in circumstances where the court considers it is likely that the person will continue to lack capacity to manage his or her own affairs after reaching the age of 18. This continues the jurisdiction of the former Court of Protection in relation to children under 16.

The relationship between 'Gillick competency' and capacity

Capacity is a legal concept defined in the Mental Capacity Act 2005. The Act has general application to persons aged 16 or over. This means that it is technically incorrect to describe children, that is any person under the age of 16, as having (or lacking) capacity. The correct question if the child is under 16 would be to ask if the child is competent to make the particular decision in question. The confusion between the terms 'competence' and 'capacity' arises because in practice the terms are often used interchangeably and Gillick competency has only been broadly defined.

The starting point in evaluating Gillick competency would be to ask whether the child achieved sufficient understanding and intelligence to enable him or her to understand fully what is proposed. If the question needs refining then the Mental Capacity Act 2005 tests detailed above should be used. Other factors must also be taken into consideration:

> 'Gillick competence' is a developmental concept and will not be lost or acquired on a day-to-day or week-to-week basis. In the case of mental disability, that disability must also be taken into account, particularly where it is fluctuating in its effect.[15]

Children under the age of 16 are otherwise excluded[16] from the provisions of the Act:

No power which a person ('D') may exercise under this Act –

(a) in relation to a person who lacks capacity, or

---

15   *Re R (A Minor) (Wardship: Medical Treatment)* [1991] 4 All ER 187–188.
16   The Mental Capacity Act 2005 creates a new criminal offence which applies to anyone caring for a person lacking capacity who ill-treats or neglects that person. The age of the victim is not specified and so could include a child. Mental Capacity Act 2005, section 44.

(b) where D reasonably thinks that a person lacks capacity,

is exercisable in relation to a person under 16.[17]

The Mental Capacity Act 2005 and those aged 16 to 18

Why does the Mental Capacity Act 2005 cover 16- to 18-year-olds?

The background to this is as follows: in putting forward recommendations for reform of the law affecting adults who lack capacity, the Law Commission[18] commented that a number of the statutory provisions in the Children Act 1989 do not apply to 16- to 18-year-olds. For example, under section 31(3) of the Children Act 1989, no care or supervision order can be made in relation to a child of 17 (16 if married). In the private law field, sections 9(6) and (7) of the Children Act 1989 prevent section 8 orders[19] from being made or continued once a child has reached 16 unless there are 'exceptional' circumstances, which would include the child's lack of capacity in relation to the matter in question.

How can the 17-year-old be protected in the community?

No care order may be made with respect to a child who has reached the age of 17, or 16 in the case of a married child.[20] A care order will continue until a child is 18 unless ended earlier.

Guidance for protecting vulnerable adults excludes any persons under the age of 18.[21]

The use of the Mental Health Act 'community orders' are restricted in the case of persons with learning disabilities by the definition of mental impairment and the restricted interpretation of the term 'seriously irresponsible' by the courts.[22]

---

17   Mental Capacity Act 2005, section 2(5).
18   The Law Commission advises the Government on the need for changes in legislation. See Law Commission Report, No. 231, paragraph 2.52.
19   Children Act 1989 section 8 orders include contact, prohibited steps, residence and specific issue orders.
20   Children Act 1989, section 31(3).
21   Home Office and Department of Health (2000) *No Secrets: Guidance on Developing and Implementing Multi-agency Policies and Procedures to Protect Vulnerable Adults from Abuse.* London: DH.
22   *Re F (Mental Health Act: Guardianship)* [2000] 1 FLR 192.

> If a vulnerable 17-year-old living in the community requires protection then decision making on behalf of that child may take place within the framework of the Mental Capacity Act 2005, but only if that young person is adjudged to lack capacity. If this statutory regime applies then application to either the Court of Protection or the children's courts can be made.[21]
>
> Even if a 17-year-old has capacity the High Court may choose to intervene if requested to exercise powers under either wardship or the inherent jurisdiction.[22]

The Law Commission concluded that, where continuing substitute decision-making arrangements are needed for someone aged 16 or 17, this was likely to be because the young person lacks mental capacity to make the decisions in question and not because he or she is under the age of legal majority. It followed that the provisions of the new capacity legislation should apply in those circumstances, and not just where there is no one available to exercise parental responsibility. For example, there may be circumstances where it is in the young person's best interests for someone other than a person with parental responsibility to be appointed as deputy to make financial or personal welfare decisions. Or, it may be appropriate for the Court of Protection to make welfare decisions, for example where the young person should live, or medical treatment decisions concerning a young person lacking capacity to consent where it is considered that those with parental responsibility are not acting in the young person's best interests.

The Mental Capacity Act 2005, therefore, introduces a parallel jurisdiction for decision making alongside the Children Act and the High Court's inherent jurisdiction in relation to young people aged 16 to 18 years.[23]

In cases where legal proceedings are required to resolve disputes or make legally effective arrangements for someone aged 16 to 18, the Law Commission decided it would not make sense to require two sets of legal proceedings to be conducted within a short period of time where the problems arising from the young person's incapacity are likely to continue after age 18. To accommodate this, the Mental Capacity Act 2005 makes provision for transfer from the Court of Protection (the decision-making judicial body on

---

23   Mental Capacity Act 2005 (Transfer of Proceedings) Order.
24   Re SA (Vulnerable Adult with Capacity: Marriage) [2006] 1 FLR 867.

behalf of people who lack capacity) to the family courts, and vice versa.[25] This means that the choice of court will depend on what is appropriate in the particular circumstances of the case. The courts are directed to take into account specific factors in deciding which court should have jurisdiction in a particular case. For example, in deciding whether to transfer a case from a court having jurisdiction under the Children Act to the Court of Protection the court must consider 'the extent to which any order made as respects a person who lacks capacity is likely to continue to have effect when that person reaches 18'.[26]

Disputes about the best interests of a young person

Decision making in relation to children aged 16 and over is covered by the Mental Capacity Act 2005. This means that the statutory framework described above must be applied to all areas of substitute decision making covered by the Act. The Act allows a decision-maker to make a decision on behalf of a person who lacks capacity in that person's best interests. The Code contains the following advice:

> Healthcare staff providing treatment, or a person providing care to the young person, can carry out treatment or care with protection from lia-bility (section 5) whether or not a person with parental responsibility consents.[27]

The Code goes on to stress that when assessing a person's best interests health care staff must take into account the views of carers 'where it is practi-cal and appropriate to do so', and this may include the young person's parents and others with parental responsibility. This guidance, although the-oretically correct, should be approached with caution. If the situation is not urgent then the views of the person with parental responsibility should be sought unless it is not in the young person's interests to do so; this might arise where abuse is suspected. In areas of doubt an application to the family courts or the Court of Protection should be considered.

---

25   Mental Capacity Act 2005, section 21.
26   Regulation 3(3)(c), The Mental Capacity Act 2005 (Transfer of Proceedings) Order (SI 2007, No. 1899).
27   Department of Constitutional Affairs (2007) *Mental Capacity Act 2005 Code of Practice.* London: TSO, paragraph 12.17

Conclusions

The Mental Capacity Act 2005 will impact on young people and children, particularly young people aged between 16 and 18. The majority of young people with complex mental health difficulties who require in-patient psychiatric treatment are likely to be treated informally.[28] Decision making on behalf of these young people, if they are over 16 and lack capacity to make such decisions for themselves, will be regulated by the MCA. If there is no person with parental responsibility, or the person with parental responsibility is not acting in the best interests of the child, the MCA provides a statutory framework setting out how decisions may be made on their behalf. The Court of Protection has an extended jurisdiction to resolve disputes. As the MCA covers decision making on personal welfare matters, as well as property, this includes medical treatment decisions. This will be particularly significant for health care professionals.

Case example

G is aged 17 and is an informal patient in a psychiatric unit. She is an asylum seeker, her parents have abandoned her and the local authority has been providing her with support and assistance. She is not subject to a care order. Professionals involved with her care and treatment have concerns about her ability to make important decisions. It is proposed that she is given medication.

How would the legal framework contained in the Mental Capacity Act frame your response? The following paragraphs provide some pointers.

The principles of the Mental Capacity Act must be followed in making decisions about her care and treatment. She must be assumed to have capacity to consent to (or refuse) any proposed treatment unless it is established that she lacks capacity. Does she lack capacity? (Is there an impairment of, or disturbance in, the functioning of mind or brain and is that disturbance sufficient to make her unable to make the decision in question?) Her ability to make the particular decision must then be evaluated; for example, can she use or weigh the information about the proposed course of treatment as part of the process of making the decision? Have

---

28 'Formal compulsion under mental health legislation is not necessarily the most prevalent route for the admission of minors'. The Tenth Biennial Report of the MHAC 2001-2003, page 247.

practicable steps been taken to assist her in making the decision, for example the provision of interpreters or an advocate? Has her right to make an unwise decision been considered?

If it is concluded that she lacks capacity to consent, the treatment must be adjudged to be in her best interests in order for the treatment providers to be protected from liability under the Mental Capacity Act. An IMCA must be appointed if there are no appropriate family or friends to represent and support her. Regard must be had to whether the purpose for which the treatment is needed can be as effectively achieved in a way that is less restrictive of the person's rights and freedom of action. For example, the advantages and disadvantages of oral medication against medication being provided by way of injection should be evaluated following this principle. In addition, all relevant factors in the best interests 'checklist' must be considered. If she is being treated following Mental Capacity Act principles the treatment providers will be protected under section 5 of the Act unless the circumstances in which the treatment is given constitute a deprivation of her liberty. So if there is a deprivation of liberty or if she is actively resisting treatment and the primary purpose of the intervention is to provide medical treatment for mental disorder, then consideration should be given to using the Mental Health Act.

Chapter 8

Service Provision and Entitlement

Introduction

Any discussion about the care and treatment of a child or young person with complex mental health difficulties will inevitably turn to the issue of 'limited resources'. These discussions can be fruitless unless they are contextualised. Is the problem in the case caused by the absence of a suitable resource or deficits in the planning process? What is the particular local context? (Each local and health authority will have developed their own arrangements to allow funding decisions to be made in complex cases.) Arguably the difficulties that arise in managing specific cases are attributable not so much to the individual's entitlement to a particular service but the organisational problems that continue to beset the assessment and planning process. In particular, assessment and planning during 'critical transitional periods',[1] in the case of many of the young people that will be between their 16th and 18th birthday, can be problematic.

All the children and young people described in this book are entitled, under a number of statutes, to both assessment and a range of services. The precise source of the child's entitlement to service may not particularly matter to the mental health professional, parent or child; what will matter is the nature of the service to be delivered, the speed with which the service can be delivered and whether there are any impediments to the successful delivery of service.

---

1   Read, J., Clements, L. and Ruebain, D. (2006) *Disabled Children and the Law*, 2nd edn. London: Jessica Kingsley Publishers, page 45.

The first part of this chapter outlines the general responsibilities imposed by statute on health and local authorities to assess and provide services. The second part outlines the organisational changes effected by the Children Act 2004. The third considers some of the responsibilities placed on local authorities under the Children Act 1989. The fourth identifies other statutes which are relevant in the context of service provision. The fifth details specific responsibilities for children in hospital. The sixth part identifies the non-statutory frameworks for the delivery of service in this area.

1 – General statutory responsibilities for assessment and provision of service

Health and local authorities are required by law to assess and, if appropriate, to provide services to certain categories of children and young people.

The NHS Act 2006[2] places a general obligation on health authorities to promote a comprehensive health service (including mental health) in their area. The courts are reluctant to interfere with the decisions made by health and local authorities in the area of what can loosely be termed 'resource allocation'.[3]

The Local Authority Social Services Act 1970 empowers local authorities to discharge their social service functions. These functions are now discharged by children's services. The Children Act 1989 imposes responsibilities on local authorities to certain categories of children – see below.

2 – Children Act 2004

The Children Act 2004 implements recommendations made following the investigations into the death of Victoria Climbié.[4] The 2004 Act contains

---

2   National Health Service Act 2006, section 1, and National Health Service (Wales) Act 2006, section 1.
3   R v. *Cambridge Health Authority ex parte B* [1995] 2 All ER 129. A similar approach by the courts can be identified in relation to decision making by local authorities; in R v. *London Borough of Barnet ex parte B* [1994] 1 FLR 592, Auld J held that the weight to be given to financial constraints when a local authority considered the range and level of day-care services for children in need in its area was a matter for the experience and judgement of the local authority and the court would rarely intervene.
4   Every Child Matters (Cm 5860) (September 2003). London: TSO.

provisions designed to improve the planning, delivery and commissioning of children's services. Section 10 of the 2004 Act, entitled 'Co-operation to Improve Well-being',[5] imposes a duty on 'each children's service authority' in England to promote cooperation with other 'partners' to improve the well-being of children relating to: physical and mental health and emotional well-being; protection from harm and neglect; education training and recreation; the contribution made by them to society; and social and economic well-being.[6] The Act provides for the establishment of local safeguarding children boards replacing area child protection committees. Section 18 of the Act requires the appointment of a director of children's services to take over the functions previously exercised by directors of education and social services.

One of the objectives of the Children Act 2004 is to allow (and require) the development of multi-agency approaches to planning and developing services for children in consultation with children and families across universal, targeted and specialist services. 'Targeted' in this context means the development of early multi-agency preventative services. In broad terms the governance structure for developing these approaches rests with children and young people's strategic partnership boards. These multi-agency boards have responsibility for strategic planning for children and this will include mental health trusts, PCTs and CAMHS. The lead agency for these boards is the local authority. The strategic priorities for children's services within a local authority, including children with mental health difficulties, are set down in children and young people's plans[7] which are required to be developed every three years.

Operational decisions about the delivery of services for individual children with complex mental health needs will vary from area to area. Some authorities (health and children's services) have piloted delivery of such services through a joint commissioning framework utilising pooled budgets to attempt to prevent children and families being passed between agencies. Within such a complex framework it is difficult to particularise

---

5   Children Act 2004, section 10. A children's service authority covers local authorities and the partners include health authorities.

6   Ibid., section 10(4).

7   Ibid., section 17. The Children and Young People's Plan (England) Regulations 2005 (SI 2005/2149) requires each children's service authority to produce a children and young people's plan setting out the authority's strategy for discharging their functions in relation to children and young people.

how practitioners and carers should deal with the organisations involved if deficit in the delivery of services becomes problematic.

The case example at the end of the chapter illustrates an approach to planning care and treatment for a young person.

3 – Local authority responsibilities under the Children Act

Part 3 of the Children Act, 'Local Authority Support for Children and Families', gives powers and duties to local authorities to provide services for children and their families, in particular to children in need.

Children in need

There is a general duty placed on local authorities to safeguard and promote the welfare of children in their area who are in need and, so far as is consistent with that duty, to promote the upbringing of such children by their families, by providing a range and level of services appropriate to those children's needs.[8] A child is in need if:

- he is unlikely to achieve or maintain, or to have the opportunity of achieving or maintaining, a reasonable standard of health or development without the provision of services by a local authority; or

- his health or development is likely to be significantly impaired or further impaired without the provision of such services;

- or if he is disabled.

The definition of a disabled child includes a child who is defined as being 'blind, deaf or dumb' or suffering 'from mental disorder of any kind'.[9] These definitions are likely to cover all the children and young people who are the subject of this book.

---

8   Children Act, section 17(1).
9   Ibid., section 17(11). Additional financial systems are in place for disabled children: section 17A.

Assessment of the child in need

Although there is no duty to assess a child in need under the Children Act 1989 equivalent to the duty found in the National Health Service and Community Care Act 1990, section 47, this will be of academic significance in relation to the cases covered by this book.

> The assessment obligation [in the Children Act 1989] is strongly reinforced by policy guidance and given the alternative rights of disabled children to an assessment under the community care legislation the CA 1989 assessment obligation must in most cases be tantamount to a public law duty.[10]

Framework for the Assessment of Children in Need and their Families details the assessment process to be followed by local authorities.[11] Time limits contained in the 'Framework for Assessment' include an initial assessment within 7 working days and a core assessment within 35 working days. A core assessment is defined as:

> an in-depth assessment which addresses the central or most important aspects of the needs of a child and the capacity of his or her care givers to respond appropriately to these needs within the wider family and community context. While this assessment is led by social services, it will invariably involve other agencies or independent professionals, who will either provide information they hold about the child or parents, contribute specialist knowledge or advice to social services or undertake specialist assessments.[12]

Services for children in need

The Children Act requires local authorities to offer the following specific services for children in need and their families:

- advice, guidance and counselling

- occupational, social, cultural and recreational activities

- care or supervised activities (including day care)

---

10   Clements, L. and Thompson, P. (2007) *Community Care and the Law*. 4th edn. London: Legal Action Group, Paragraph 24.13.
11   Department of Health (2000) *Framework for the Assessment of Children in Need and their Families*. London: DH.
12   Ibid., paragraph 3.11.

- home help
- travel assistance
- holiday
- maintenance of the family home
- financial help
- provision of family accommodation.[13]

Looked after and accommodated children

The Children Act introduces two concepts: 1. children being looked after by a local authority and 2 children being provided with accommodation.

All children being looked after are either in care under a care order or being provided with accommodation. For example, a child subject to a secure accommodation order under section 25 who is not subject to a care order is therefore being provided with accommodation

Complaints

Every local authority must establish a procedure for considering represen-tations and complaints by or on behalf of a child regarding the provisions of services under Part 3 of the Act.[14] This will include, therefore, both complaints concerning accommodation and complaints about the range of services (see list above) provided by the local authority. If the complaint concerns the provision of services under the Act then an independent person must be appointed to oversee the investigation. All children involved in the complaints process have a statutory right to an advocate.[15]

---

13   This list is taken from Hershman, D. and McFarlane, A. (2007) *Children, Law and Practice.* Family Law, paragraphs 56–75, Division G Local Authority Responsibility.
14   Children Act, section 26(3).
15   Adoption and Children Act 2002, section 119, inserting section 26A into the Children Act 1989.

The provision of accommodation

Where a child is in care the local authority, who have responsibility for him under a care order, must provide accommodation. Even if a child is not subject to a care order, local authorities have a duty to provide accommodation for a child in need where there is no one with parental responsibility for him, he is lost or abandoned, the person caring for him is prevented from providing him with suitable accommodation or care, he is over 16 and the local authority considers his welfare is likely to be seriously prejudiced without the provision of accommodation.[16]

The transition into adulthood

Although in general services under the Children Act cease to be available at the age of 18, there are exceptions. The Act specifically provides power to the local authority to provide accommodation for a person between the ages of 16 and 21 in a community home if it would safeguard or promote his welfare.[17] Under amendments to the Children Act made by the Children (Leaving Care) Act 2000 certain categories of young people who have been looked after will be entitled to ongoing assistance until they reach 21.

Consulting the child and their families

The Children Act 2004, section 53, amends the Children Act 1989 to provide that:

> Before determining what (if any) services to provide for a particular child in need in the exercises of functions conferred on them by this section, a local authority shall, so far as is reasonably practicable and consistent with the child's welfare:
>
> (a) ascertain the child's wishes and feelings regarding the provision of those services; and
>
> (b) give due consideration (having regard to his age and understanding) to such wishes and feelings of the child as they have been able to ascertain.

---

16   Children Act, section 20. The Act also provides that a local authority may provide accommodation for other children and young adults.

17   Ibid., section 20(5).

Guidance to health authorities underlines the need to improve participation and user involvement, particularly in relation to the mental health needs of minority communities.[18]

4 – Other statutory provisions

Carers' legislation

Various statutes place responsibilities on local authorities to assess, and to make provision for, parents and others who are providing (or intending to provide) regular and substantial unpaid care for a disabled child.[19]

The Mental Health Act 1983

Children and young people who are detained under section 3 of the Mental Health Act 1983 (or under a section 37 hospital order), and who cease to be detained and leave hospital, are entitled to after-care services provided under section 117. This section places a duty on a primary care trust or health authority and on a local social services authority to provide 'after-care services' until such time as they are satisfied there is no longer the need. Section 117 services must be provided free of charge.[20]

A child or young person with complex mental health difficulties living in the community will therefore have rights under the Children Act 1989 as a child in need and rights under other community care legislation. If in hospital they have general rights under the NHS Act and following discharge specific rights to services if they have been detained under sections 3, 37, 45A, 47 or 48 of the Mental Health Act 1983.

---

18   Department of Health (2004) *The National Service Framework for Children, Young People and Maternity Services: The Mental Health and Psychological Well-being of Children and Young People*. London: DH, pages 13–14.

19   Disabled Persons (Services, Consultation and Representation) Act 1986, Carers (Recognition and Services) Act 1995, the Carers and Disabled Children Act 2000 and the Carers (Equal Opportunities) Act 2004.

20   *R* v. *Manchester City Council ex parte Stennett* [2002] 4 All ER 124.

5 – Specific responsibilities to children in hospitals

Children accommodated by health authorities

The Children Act 1989[21] places a responsibility on NHS trusts, health and education authorities, residential care homes and nursing and mental nursing homes (private hospitals) to inform the local authority if they have accommodated a child[22] for more than three months, or are intending to do so. The local authority must:

(a) Take such steps as are reasonably practicable to enable them to determine whether the child's welfare is adequately safeguarded and promoted while he is accommodated by the accommodating authority; and

(b) Consider the extent to which (if at all) they should exercise any of their functions under this Act [Children Act] with respect to the child.[23]

The purpose of this section is to:

ensure that children are not 'forgotten' and that SSDs assess the quality of the child care offered. Children with disabilities are more likely than other children to be placed in 'out of county' placements, frequently in remote and rural areas. The new arrangements should ensure more coherent planning for children and will necessitate close collaboration with child health services...[24]

Education in hospitals

Current government policy in relation to education for children and young people in psychiatric units and hospitals states as follows:

---

21   Children Act 1989, sections 85 and 86.
22   By virtue of the Children Act 1989, section 24(2)(d), a person under the age of 21 who was, at any time after reaching the age of 16 but whilst still a child, accommodated but is no longer accommodated qualifies for advice and assistance under section 24.
23   Children Act 1989, section 85(4).
24   The Children Act 1989 Guidance and Regulations, Volume 6, Children with Disabilities (1991). London: HMSO, paragraph 13.10. Also see: *Too Serious a Thing. The Review of Safeguards for Children and Young People Treated and Cared for by the NHS in Wales* (2002). The Carlile Review. Cardiff: National Assembly for Wales, paragraph 5.11.

A small number of young people develop severe emotional and behavioural disorders, which require care and treatment beyond that which can be found in school, or sometimes even in local health care. Some of these young people need special boarding schools while others need to be treated in hospital. Some are placed in NHS or private mental health units or hospitals. Pupils placed in such units retain an entitlement to education. Private mental health units must plan with the LEA [now children's services] to ensure that pupils who are mental health patients continue to access their entitlement to education. [25]

The importance of education in an in-patient setting is established. [26] It follows that when planning for the transition from hospital to the community returning to education should be one of the important factors to be taken into account when assessing the needs of the particular child.

Responsibilities of hospital managers for child in-patients

To ensure compliance with section 116 of the Mental Health Act 1983 and sections 85 and 86 of the Children Act 1989:

- where a child is subject to a care order the relevant local authority should be contacted on the child's admission and reminded of their responsibilities under section 116, and

- the three-month period for a section 85/86 notification should be recorded following the admission of any child as an in-patient to prevent the notification requirements being overlooked.

Welfare of certain hospital patients

Section 116 of the Mental Health Act 1983 is entitled 'Welfare of Certain Hospital Patients'. The section applies to children subject to care orders who are 'admitted to a hospital, independent hospital or care home in England and Wales (whether for treatment for mental disorder or for any other reason)'. [27]

---

25   Department for Education and Skills (2001) *Access to Education for Children and Young People with Medical Needs*. LAC (2001) 27, page 7, paragraph 1.13.

26   French, W. and Tate, A. (1998) 'Educational Management.' In: *In-patient Child Psychiatry*. London: Routledge, pages 143–155.

27   Mental Health Act 1983, section 116(1).

This section is not limited to psychiatric hospitals and will cover children receiving medical treatment for any condition in an NHS or private hospital. The section requires the local authority designated in the care order to arrange for visits to be made and 'shall take such other steps in relation to the patient while in the hospital, independent hospital or care home as would be expected to be taken by his parents'.

This could, for example, be used to ensure that a child does not lose contact with the wider family by organising and funding visits from family members, promoting continuing contact and links with the wider community and arranging for the provision of an advocate.

6 – Frameworks for the delivery of service

The Care Programme Approach (CPA)

The delivery of all specialist mental health services is framed within the CPA.[28] *Building Bridges*, published in 1995, states that the CPA is the cornerstone of the government's mental health policy[29] and provides detailed guidance about the operation of the CPA. Some requirements of the CPA were modified in 1999. These modifications are contained in a booklet entitled *Effective Care Co-ordination in Mental Health Services – Modernising the Care Programme Approach*.[30] *Refocusing the Care Programme Approach* states that from October 2008 the term the 'Care Programme Approach' will only be applied to those individuals (including children and young people) with complex needs.[31]

The CPA applies to people under the care of the secondary mental health service (health and social care) regardless of setting. The four main elements to the CPA (as modified in 1999) include: systematic assessment of

---

28   HC(90)23/LASSL(90)11 and in the Welsh Office (1995) *Mental Illness Strategy* (WHC(95)40).

29   Department of Health (1995) *Building Bridges – A Guide to Arrangements for Inter-agency Working for the Care and Protection of Severely Mentally Ill People.* London: DH, paragraph 3.0.3.

30   Department of Health (2001) *Effective Care Co-ordination in Mental Health Services – Modernising the Care Programme Approach.* London: DH.

31   'In the main, the individuals needing the support of (new) CPA should not be significantly different from those currently needing the support of enhanced CPA. The current characteristics of those needing enhanced CPA are described as individuals who need: multi-agency support; active engagement; intense intervention; support with dual diagnoses; and who are at higher risk.' Department of Health (2008) *Refocusing the Care Programme Approach: Policy and Positive Practice Guidance.* London: DH.

the patient's needs, formation of a care plan to address those needs, appointment of a care coordinator and regular review and changes to the care plan
where necessary. The CPA itself applies to adults of working age but the
principles are expected to be applied to children and young people. The CPA
is currently under review by the Department of Health, the results of which
have not yet been published.

A child who is eligible for the CPA is also likely to have been assessed
under the Framework for the Assessment of Children in Need and their
Families (see above). This overlap can present practical problems as the CPA
care coordinator may not be familiar with the common assessment framework and the CAMHS professionals may not be familiar with the application of the CPA. Where there is overlap it must be the responsibility of the
CPA care coordinator to ensure that services are properly delivered.[32] The
importance of the care coordinator should not be underestimated:

> When we bear in mind the difficulties that parents and children have in
> obtaining comprehensive and reliable information, as well as accessing
> complex, fragmented and uncoordinated services, it is hardly surprising
> that research has emphasised repeatedly that one of the most valued
> provisions is the allocation of a particular worker to parents and their
> children.[33]

The National Service Framework (NSF)

The National Service Framework for Children, Young People and Maternity
Services establishes standards for promoting the health and well-being of
children and young people and for providing services. Standard 9 deals with
the 'Mental Health and Psychological Well-being of Children and Young
People'.[34] Standard 9 links the CPA with the provision of services to children
and young people:

---

32 See 'Annex B: CPA and Child and Adolescent Mental Health Services' in Department of
    Health (2008) *Refocusing the Care Programme Approach: Policy and Positive Practice Guidance*.

33 Read, J., Clements, L. and Ruebain, D. (2006) *Disabled Children and the Law*, 2nd edn.
    London: Jessica Kingsley Publishers, page 59.

34 Department of Health (2004) *The National Service Framework for Children, Young People and
    Maternity Services: The Mental Health and Psychological Well-being of Children and Young
    People*. London: DH.

When children and young people are discharged from in-patient services into the community and when young people are transferred from child to adult services, their continuity of care is ensured by use of the 'care programme approach'.[35]

Conclusions

There are a number of potential fault lines at both a local and national level that can be identified in relation to the delivery of services to children and young people with complex mental health difficulties. These include: the need for urgent and specialist mental health assessments, the need for age-appropriate accommodation, the need for effective planning when children and young people are to be transferred and discharged from in-patient services and the particular difficulties in planning for young people aged between 16 and 18.

The young people who experience these difficulties are likely to be adolescents undergoing huge changes in their lives. This means that planning for their needs must accommodate these rapid changes and a focus on effective care coordination should help young people to move on in as stable a manner as possible.

Although the law requires the many statutory authorities involved in the planning and delivery of services to children and young people with complex mental health difficulties to cooperate, this sometimes does not take place. When this occurs then internal complaints processes may have to be initiated, with the primary focus of the complaint being the failure of the authorities to work together as required by statute.[36]

Case example

George developed mental health problems when he was 13. When he was aged 15 he was admitted to Seacrest, a specialist adolescent unit which does not have a high dependency unit. He was diagnosed as suffering from a bipolar disorder with psychotic symptoms. He displayed chaotic behaviour, mood swings and

---

35   Ibid., page 5, paragraph 10.
36   Read, J., Clements, L. and Ruebain, D. (2006) *Disabled Children and the Law*, 2nd edition. London: Jessica Kingsley Publishers, page 45 and Appendix 1, 'Complaints Material', page 59.

physical aggression. He was treated at Seacrest for ten months. He was then discharged home to the care of his parents. A month later, unknown to his parents, he left home and he was found wandering in a confused state near an inter-city railway line. He was arrested by police on a section 136 and admitted to an adult psychiatric ward. The decision to admit him to an adult ward was made for a number of reasons. First, George is tall and looks mature for his age and was carrying no ID. Although his parents had reported him missing it took some time to confirm his identity. Second, he was arrested at the start of bank holiday weekend.

After five days he was transferred back to Seacrest where he remained for some eight weeks. His condition deteriorated. A decision was then made that he should be detained in hospital under section 3 of the Mental Health Act. The statutory procedures were followed, George was detained, but because Seacrest did not have a high dependency unit he was then transferred to a specialist private hospital. After three months his condition had appeared to stabilise, although his behaviour remained intermittently challenging, and he was not consistently compliant with treatment.

The team responsible for his in-patient care arranged a section 117 meeting. A psychiatrist from Seacrest and a psychologist from George's CAMHS team attended the meeting. A social worker from George's home local authority was not able to attend. George's mother had told all the professionals involved that she could no longer cope with him at home, and she was not prepared to have him back. As he was now aged 16 a discharge plan was developed outlining two types of community provision that could meet George's needs: a foster placement or a residential unit. A particular therapeutic unit was identified. This unit is in another part of the country from where George was living.

George just wants to get out of hospital and has applied to a Mental Health Review Tribunal. The following problems have now arisen in relation to discharge planning: it is proving difficult to get the assessment of his needs, and the discharge plan to support that assessment, agreed. Particular problems have emerged including: an absence of any agreement about funding a placement in a therapeutic community for George and to obtain any agreement from the CAMHS team local to the therapeutic community to take over George's case. George must have a GP in order to be discharged and have a community placement, but the GPs will not register him because he does not yet have an address.

What steps could be taken to progress George's transition into the community?

Planning for George

A multi-agency planning meeting chaired by a senior manager from either children's services or the health authority should be arranged. Prior to the meeting taking place the team responsible for George's care should prepare a clearly worked plan covering the following areas:

1.   What are George's needs based on the multi-disciplinary assessments conducted to date?

2.   Is there any possibility of George returning home to live with his parents with support for him and his family?

3.   If George cannot go home what type of placement does he require? For example, is it a specialist placement with specialist health provision, a specialist social service placement or a specialist foster placement?

4.   Once a placement has been identified that best meets George's needs, the health commissioners will need to discuss and agree funding for the placement with the children's service commissioners. Many local authorities have created joint funding panels involving both health and children's services.

Identifying the type of support that George will need when he leaves hospital will obviously depend on whether he returns home, or the type and location of the placement away from home that has been identified.[37] Planning for his support after he leaves hospital will need to involve the CAMHS team local to his placement.

George will be entitled to a care coordinator. That person should be appointed within a short time of his admission to hospital and that person should be involved in the pre-discharge planning process.

---

37   Guidance in relation to commissioning 'out of area' placements is contained in Department of Health (2007) *Who Pays? Establishing the Responsible Commissioner.* London: DH, paragraph 30.

Part 2

Practice Issues

Chapter 9

The Role and Function of the Approved Social Worker/Approved Mental Health Professional

Introduction

This chapter is written by Wendy Whitaker, a practising approved social worker (ASW). The chapter lists the role and function of the ASW and illustrates some practice dilemmas by way of various case examples. There is some overlap between this chapter and Chapters 4 and 5.

As already stated in the preface to this book during the course of publication the Mental Health Act 2007 became law. This requires that consideration is given to the role of the successor to the ASW, the Approved Mental Health Professional (AMHP). AMHPs will replace ASWs on 1 October 2008. The statutory functions of ASWs when they become AMHPs will be expanded insofar as they will have specific functions in relation to CTOs.

It is anticipated that all existing ASWs will be accredited to become AMHPs following the provision of training. This chapter, therefore, continues to refer in the main to ASWs except where it is appropriate to either refer to ASW/ AMHPs or AMHPs alone.

The Mental Health Act 2007 has extended the range of professionals able to undertake the functions previously performed by an ASW. AMHPs will be drawn from the following professions:

- social workers

- first level nurses, their field of practice being mental health or learning disabilities nursing
- occupational therapists
- chartered psychologists.

Whilst local social services authorities will no longer have to employ AMHPs they will continue to be responsible for approving AMHPs in the same way as they did for ASWs.

Partnership – medical recommendations, the ASW and the nearest relative

The partnership between the two doctors providing the medical recommendations, the ASW and the nearest relative is central to the assessment. Each is necessarily independent; however, good communication, cooperation and mutual support between all three participants enables a thorough assessment, militates against the negative impact for the patient and, importantly, reduces the risk of harm to all concerned.

The ASW plays a pivotal role within the Mental Health Act. If a person is to be deprived of their liberty, without scrutiny by the courts at the time of application, then one of the ASW's functions is to be a 'rights protector', that is providing independent specialist input into the assessment process from a social care rather than medical perspective. At present the ASW's involvement under the Mental Health Act 1983 is very much at the stage of compelling the patient into hospital and there is little formal contact thereafter. The additional roles imposed on AMHPs by the Mental Health Act 2007, (see below) will change this.

What are the checks and balances to prevent injustice?

- Historically the independence of the ASW has related to their employment by the local authority and not by the NHS. This has now been changed by the Mental Health Act 2007. Whether this independence, which has been traditionally linked with their employment arrangements, will change remains to be seen. Arguably their independence is more likely to be preserved by their continuing status as a cadre of professionals with specific statutory functions working within a culture distinct from the culture of other health professionals.

Although AMHPs act on behalf of a LSSA [local social service authority], they do so as independent professionals and must exercise their own judgement based on social and medical evidence when deciding whether to apply for a patient to be brought under the statutory powers of the Act. The role of the AMHP is to provide an independent decision about whether there are alternatives to detention under the Act or not, bringing a social care perspective to their decision.[1]

- The right of the nearest relative, particularly the right of the nearest relative to request an assessment by an ASW of the need for a patient to be detained in hospital, can be interpreted as a counterweight to the power of the ASW.

A good working relationship between the professionals involved requires them to have an understanding of each other's respective roles and responsibilities.

When the ASW should be involved

The ASW should be consulted when an assessment for detention is being considered. The reason for this is because they have a wide role, both to prevent the necessity for compulsory admission to hospital, the 'least restrictive alternative', as well as making the application where they decide it is appropriate.[2]

If a decision not to detain a patient is made there needs to be a clear alternative plan to manage risk. The reasons for not detaining need to be detailed in writing in the medical notes by the ASW. In addition the nearest relative needs to be informed of the alternative plan, which may involve supporting them as carers.

---

1 Department of Health (2007) *Mental Health Act 1983 Draft revised Code of Practice.* London: DH, paragraph 4.44.

2 Department of Health (1999) *Mental Health Act 1983 Code of Practice.* London: DH, paragraph 2.11, and DHSS circular, LAC (86)15. The 2007 Draft Code contains a number of guiding principles including the 'least restrictive alternative principle.' Department of Health (2007) *Mental Health Act 1983 Draft revised Code of Practice.* London: DH, paragraph 1.3.

ASW responsibilities

The ASW has the responsibility for coordinating the assessment and admission to hospital of the patient.

> Unless different arrangements have been agreed locally between the relevant authorities, AMHPs assessing patients for possible admission under the Act have overall responsibility for co-ordinating the process of assessment, and, when they decide to make an application, for implementing that decision.[3]

This can often be difficult and time-consuming. The ASW needs to organise two medical recommendations. One should be a doctor who knows the patient, ideally the patient's GP, otherwise the ASW needs to organise a second section 12 approved doctor. The ASW also needs to arrange for the attendance of the police if there is concern regarding potential risk, which may not always be apparent, and an ambulance to convey the patient.

Case 1

A pregnant young person, H (aged 16), is living alone on the third floor of a block of flats with no lift. Her psychotic illness has been managed in the community to avoid admitting her to an adult acute ward. When she refuses access to the domiciliary midwife the ASW arranges for a Mental Health Act assessment. Through a half-open door, and with persuasion, she agrees to allow access to the ASW and the GP as she knows both professionals. The police are on the scene but maintain a discreet distance. On seeing other people (the second opinion doctor and another social worker) H slams the door shut.

If it is not possible to persuade her to open the door what would be the legal authority to force entry?

Ideally there should be a pre-meeting between all professionals involved to discuss and coordinate the section assessment and plan for problematic outcomes.

---

3   Department of Health (2007) *Mental Health Act 1983 Draft revised Code of Practice.* London: DH, paragraph 4.42.

ASW responsibilities and the nearest relative

The ASW is required by the Act to attempt to identify the patient's nearest relative as defined in section 26 of the Act and must ensure that the statutory obligations with respect of the nearest relative set out in section 11 of the Act are fulfilled. (These functions remain the responsibility of the AMHP after 1 October 2008.) When doing so, the AMHP should, where possible:

- ascertain the nearest relative's views about both the patient's needs and the nearest relative's own needs in relation to the patient; and

- inform the nearest relative of the reasons for considering an application for admission to hospital under the Act and the effects of making such an application.[4]

This includes using the list contained in the Mental Health Act[5] and then identifying whether or not the person is over 18, if they are caring for the person and if there is more than one who is the oldest.

Before making the application the ASW must interview the patient in a 'suitable manner'.[6] The ASW must have personally seen the patient within 14 days ending on the date of the application.[7]

In relation to a section 2 application the ASW must, before or within a reasonable time after an application, take such steps as are practicable to inform the person appearing to be the nearest relative that the application is to be or has been made.[8] The ASW must consult with the nearest relative before making an application under section 3 unless such consultation is not reasonably practicable or would involve unreasonable delay. The nearest relative is entitled to object to an application under section 3, which cannot then be made unless the nearest relative were to be displaced by the county court.

The duty to consult or inform the nearest relative was considered in the case of *E* v. *Bristol City Council*.[9] In this case the patient did not wish her sister (her nearest relative) to be consulted by the ASW. Bennett J analysed the case both in relation to domestic and human rights law. In relation to the former he concluded that the word 'practicability' contained in the MHA required the ASW to take into account the consequences of consultation, that is in this

---

4   Ibid., paragraph 4.48.
5   Mental Health Act 1983, section 26.
6   Ibid., section 13(2).
7   Ibid., section 11(5).
8   Ibid., section 11(3).
9   *E* v. *Bristol City Council* [2005] EWHC 74.

case it would have distressed the patient. In relation to the application of Article 8 he decided the patient's Article 8 rights had either been interfered with or were in 'real danger' of being interfered with. He decided that he could interpret the word 'practicable' to take into account the patient's wishes. This judgment therefore places an onus on the ASW to consider the consequences of consultation, and there will be some circumstances where they will decide not to consult or inform, for example where the patient has been abused by their nearest relative.

Case 2

V is 17. She is accommodated by the local authority. She has been treated by professionals from her local CAMHS for some months, and recently has been staying as an in-patient during the week at a specialist psychiatric unit. Her mental health is now rapidly deteriorating. She has been placed on a section 2 of the Mental Health Act. However, her symptoms are not responding to treatment and it is agreed that she should now be placed on a section 3. When V was first accommodated she alleged that her father had abused both her and her sister. V understands her legal position and she is adamant that she does not want the ASW to speak to her father, who is her nearest relative. She also does not want the ASW to have any contact with her mother, who V says is colluding with her father. The prospect of the ASW talking to her father appears to be causing V distress. V's father is aware of all the allegations made by his daughter. He is apparently philosophical about these allegations, stating that they are a consequence of her illness and that she urgently needs treatment. He insists that it is his right as her nearest relative to be consulted and makes it plain that he will complain if he is not consulted.

Can V's wishes be respected?

If the nearest relative objects to a section 3 the ASW cannot proceed with the application unless the nearest relative is displaced under section 29 of the Mental Health Act. If the nearest relative is displaced, the court may appoint another relative or a member of the social services department to act as the nearest relative. It is important that the consequences of displacement are explained to the nearest relative as this may affect their approach. When operational from 1 October 2008 the new ground for displacement introduced by the Mental Health Act 2007 will also have to be explained.

A nearest relative may authorise another person to perform the functions of a nearest relative.

Case 3

A has three children. When his oldest child, Z, attains the age of 18 he becomes his father's nearest relative. Within the family's culture A's great uncle is regarded as having authority to make all decisions affecting individual family members. Z wishes to delegate his rights under the Mental Health Act to the uncle.

Can Z delegate these rights? If so, what procedures need to be followed? If not, what other course of action would help?

It is important to note that a person who has parental responsibility may not necessarily be the nearest relative of the child.

Case 4

G, a 15-year-old, lives with his mother who has parental responsibility. His father, who is older than G's mother, also has parental responsibility for G but is now separated from G's mother and lives elsewhere. He does, however, have regular contact with his son.

Who is G's nearest relative and what are the reasons for the answer?

Interview in a suitable manner

Unless there are good reasons for undertaking separate assessments, assessment should be carried out jointly by the ASW and doctor(s). The ASW must discuss the case with at least one doctor.

> It is essential that at least one of the doctors undertaking the medical assessment discussed the patient with the applicant (ASW or nearest relative) and desirable for both of them to do this.[10]

The ASW must identify themselves and other professionals and, unless there are issues of risk, explain the purpose of the interview and generally see the patient on their own.

---

10   Department of Health (1999) *The Mental Health Act 1983 Code of Practice*. London: DH, paragraph 2.3. Compare with the 2007 Draft Code: 'Unless there is good reason for undertaking separate assessments, assessments should where possible be carried out jointly by the AMHP and at least one of the two doctors involved in the assessment.'

> The patient should ordinarily be given the opportunity of speaking to the ASW alone but if the ASW has reason to fear physical harm, he or she should insist that another professional be present.[11]

If the person is drunk or drugged the ASW must return when they are sober. If issues of risk prevent this, the ASW needs to use all other information to make a decision and note the circumstances in their report.

The ASW must attempt to overcome all barriers to communication by avoiding jargon, and where necessary using translators or signers.

In summary a list of the factors that need to be taken into consideration when making the assessment include:

- the statutory criteria

- the patient's wishes and views of his or her needs

- the patient's social and family circumstances

- the nature of the illness/behaviour disorder and its cause

- the views of relatives, friends and other professionals and assessing the reliability of the information they provide

- the needs of the patient's family or others with whom they live

- the need for others to be protected from the patient

- the burden on others close to the patient of a decision not to admit.

Case 5

L is aged 15. She is suffering from anorexia, and her medical risk is increasing. She is refusing to be admitted to hospital. She seems to have insight into her illness and says that she is able to increase her food intake. On further enquiry it transpires she has not eaten, only drank, for the last four days. All the professionals responsible for her care and treatment consider that it is necessary for her to be treated as an in-patient. L's parents do not want to upset her but are very worried about her condition. They have therefore decided to consent to her admission.

---

11   Department of Health (1999) *Mental Health Act 1983 Code of Practice.* London: DH, paragraph 2.13. This guidance is largely replicated in the 2007 Draft Code. Department of Health (2007) *Mental Health Act 1983 Draft revised Code of Practice.* London: DH, paragraph 4.45.

What factors are relevant to deciding whether L should be admitted informally or detained under the Mental Health Act 1983? Would it make any difference if she were aged 16?

Throughout the interview there needs to be a balance between a full risk assessment, which may involve detailed and lengthy discussion, and, for example, the necessity for a quick decision when the risk to both the person and their family and professionals involved is an issue.

Interviewing a young person

It is important to use age-appropriate language to interview the young person, with and without their carers or other advocates, and at a pace that allows them to express themselves. This will involve giving them breaks with an aim to reducing the stress of the situation.

This may be the young person's first experience of the Mental Health Act and may therefore have long-term implications for their involvement with mental health services. For young people, social, family and personal factors are particularly important. For example, separation from family, education and peers may have a profound long-term impact on the person's social and educational achievement as well as their mental health.

The impact of the stigma of being seen as 'mad' has well-documented consequences on a person's mental well-being.[12] Detaining a young person may have implications for their sense of control and self-worth and may decrease their self-esteem.

The parents' authority and ability to care for their child may be undermined both by the young person, as a consequence of their mental health problems, but also by professionals removing a child from their care. Consideration of relying on parental consent to treatment and the use of the Mental Health Act needs to be constantly under review. The ASW needs to maintain the ability to collaborate with parents and to make an accurate assessment of the mental health needs of the young person and their carers' ability to meet these needs.

Timing may be critical; a young person may be becoming psychiatrically unwell but the parents feel able to cope. If the ASW were to make the application too soon, future collaboration regarding after-care with the parents may

---

12   Thornicroft, G. (2006) *Actions Speak Louder: Tackling Discrimination Against People with Mental Illness.* London: Mental Health Foundation.

be jeopardised. On the other hand, the parents may welcome the use of the Mental Health Act to ensure treatment, thus avoiding conflict between child and the parents as the authority to treat lies with the RMO.

The need for specialist input?

Where a patient is known to belong to a group for which particular expertise is desirable (for example, they are a young person or someone with a learning disability), at least one of the professionals involved in their assessment should have expertise in working with people from that group wherever possible. If, in exceptional circumstances, this is not (or not immediately) possible, at least one of the professionals involved in the person's assessment should, if at all possible, consult with one or more practitioners who have relevant expertise and involve them as closely as the circumstances of the case allow.[13]

Issues the ASW must consider

The ASW's role is to know what alternative services are available and how to mobilise them. All alternative therapeutic avenues must have been tried or considered, such as:

- working with a young person's carers to enable them to support the person in the community alongside schools and voluntary agencies
- considering the involvement of primary care and social services to provide additional family support
- CPNs or crisis intervention in the home environment
- out-patient and day care support
- informal admission. Informal admission may be achieved by allowing the young person to visit the in-patient unit prior to their admission and responding to their anxieties and fears.

Sectioning somebody should not be a short cut because the patient has not turned up for out-patients. Successive non-attendance at review appoint-

---

13   Department of Health (2007) *Draft revised Mental Health Act 1983 Code of Practice*. London: DH, paragraph 4.35.

ments may mean the client is managing their illness and getting on with their lives. A first step could be to contact carers to see if they have concerns. Alternatively, a crisis intervention team could be used to ensure medication compliance and offer daily support to both client and family to alleviate a full-blown relapse.

Decisions for the ASW

As well as the statutory criteria the ASW must be satisfied that:

> detention in hospital is in all the circumstances of the case the most appropriate way of providing the care and medical treatment of which the patient stands in need.[14]

Case 6

A 15-year-old patient, J, is being treated for severe anorexia nervosa. His parents are adamant that he should not be detained and he is therefore being treated on an in-patient basis with their consent. J frequently runs away from the ward to exercise. He is violent to others, throwing things at them to get them out of his way, and he is a risk to himself due to weight loss. The nurses have locked the door to restrict J's movements.

Does J need to be detained under the Mental Health Act?

ASW tasks once the application is made

The ASW should check that all the legal documents have been completed appropriately. Although this is the responsibility of the hospital managers, given that the application has to be 'founded on the written recommendations of two [doctors]'[15] the ASW needs to check their accuracy in terms of fundamentals. Common errors include:

- The medical recommendations and applications are not signed and dated.

- They do not have the correct name of the patient.

---

14   Mental Health Act 1983, section 13(2).
15   Ibid., section 3(3).

- The medical recommendations for section 3 must also include at least one of the same diagnosis.

- The application must also be to the correct hospital where the patient is being received into a bed.

The ASW has the powers of a constable to convey a patient to hospital.[16] This means the ASW may accompany the patient in the ambulance or at the very least ensure that those authorised to convey the patient have the application form and medical recommendations.[17] The ASW also has the responsibility[18] of ensuring that children, pets and property are cared for or secured. This may involve coordination with the children's social services team.

After arranging for the patient's admission to hospital the ASW:

should leave an outline report at the hospital when the patient is admitted, giving reasons for the admission and any practical matters about the patient's circumstances which the hospital should know...[19]

Other ASW tasks

The Mental Health Act provides authority for an ASW[20] to enter and inspect premises where there is reasonable cause to believe that a patient is not under proper care. However, the ASW cannot use force unless they have a section 135 warrant which allows the police to gain entry to search and remove a patient to a place of safety.

If a person has been arrested under section 136 and is taken to a place of safety, there is no requirement for the ASW to wait for a doctor to see the patient. Even if the doctor does see the patient and decides not to make a recommendation the ASW must still see the patient (for example, to explore alternative needs such as housing or finance), unless there is no evidence of mental disorder at all.[21]

---

16 Ibid., sections 6 and 137.
17 Department of Health (2007) *Mental Health Act 1983 Draft revised Code of Practice*. London: DH, paragraphs 10.21–10.22.
18 National Assistance Act 1948, section 48.
19 Department of Health (1999) *Mental Health Act 1983 Code of Practice*. London: DH, paragraph 11.13. This guidance is replicated in the 2007 Draft Code.
20 Mental Health Act, section 115.
21 Department of Health (1999) *Mental Health Act 1983 Code of Practice*. London: DH, paragraph 10.8(a).

Community treatment orders

A CTO cannot be made by a responsible clinician unless an AMHP states in writing that he agrees with the responsible clinician's opinion and it is appropriate to make the order.[22] In making the decision the Code advises that the:

> In making the decision the Code advises that the:

> AMHP should ensure that they consider the wider social context for the person concerned. For example, any support networks the patient may have, the potential impact on the rest of the patient's family and other family-related matters, employment issues and so on may be relevant. The AMHP should also ensure the cultural background and nature of the patient's family and other support structures are taken into consideration.[23]

The Mental Health Act 2007 creates a number of new functions for the AMHP in relation to CTOs. These functions are as follows:

- Before a CTO may be made, an AMHP, acting on behalf of a local social service authority, must agree with the responsible clinician's opinion that all the criteria for making the order are met and agree that it is appropriate to make the order.

- The AMHP must agree to the inclusion of any conditions (apart from the 'mandatory conditions') which the responsible clinician considers are necessary and meet the statutory criteria.

- If the responsible clinician decides that grounds for revoking the CTO are met then the AMHP must agree.

- If the responsible clinician wants to extend a CTO, and considers that the criteria are met, then an AMHP must agree that that the criteria are met and that it is appropriate to extend the CTO.

---

22   Mental Health Act 2007, section 17A(4)(b)(i) and (ii).
23   Department of Health (2007) *Mental Health Act 1983 Draft revised Code of Practice*. London: DH, paragraph 28.10.

Chapter 10

The Diagnosis and Management of Complex Mental Illness in Young People

Introduction

This chapter is written by Dr Mary Mitchell, a practising child and adolescent psychiatrist. The first part of the chapter briefly describes the structure of service delivery for young people with mental health difficulties. The second part deals with the classification of complex mental illness and some of the treatment options that are available. The third part outlines some of the diagnoses applied to the children and young people who may require in-patient treatment for mental disorder and some of the problems that they face; this then links with the various case examples presented.

1 – The four-tier model

The range of mental health services available to children and young people is described as if structured in a framework of four tiers. The first tier includes all professionals who have opportunities to support a young person with mental health needs, for example a general practitioner, teacher, school nurse or social worker. Services at Tier 4 provide the most specialist interventions, usually on a regional basis, and include in-patient services and day services for those young people with the most severe psychiatric problems.

- Tier 1: non-specialist interventions at primary level.

- Tier 2: professionals with qualifications in child mental health providing therapy on an individual basis.

- Tier 3: specialist multi-disciplinary services for the severe and complex cases.

- Tier 4: day units, highly specialised out-patient teams and in-patient units including forensic and secure units.

As originally envisaged the tier model was not supposed to be a rigid definition of service provision. An individual professional or service might be working flexibly across all levels when managing any one case. For example, a community-based drop-in counselling service for young people might see a depressed, self-harming, substance-abusing young person at high risk of self-harm who would not accept referral on to a mental health service. In a case like this a Tier 1 professional would be working with a high level of complexity and risk in consultation with colleagues in Tiers 2 and 3.

Within a typical adolescent mental health service, professionals work across Tiers 2 and 3 and also support young people admitted to and discharged from Tier 4 services. This chapter focuses on young people receiving care and treatment primarily from Tier 3 and 4 services.

2 – The spectrum of mental disorder in young people

The definition of childhood psychiatric disorder is difficult to determine. Included in these disorders are unusual behaviours, emotions or thought processes which are prolonged or severe. An essential factor is that such difficulties interfere with the young person's functioning in everyday life or within the family. The young person's stage of development and socio-cultural context will determine to some extent the degree of any disorder. During any period of one year, 10 per cent of the childhood population has mental disorder and this prevalence is similar to that in the adult population.[1]

Disorders can be divided into three main groups: emotional disorders (e.g. depression, anxiety, psychosis), disruptive behaviour disorders (e.g.

---

1   Pearce, J. (1993) 'Identifying Psychiatric Disorders in Children.' In E. Garralda (ed.) *Managing Children with Psychiatric Problems*. London: BMJ Publishing Group.

hyperactivity, conduct disorder) and developmental disorders (e.g. autistic spectrum disorders, mental retardation, language delay).[2]

In a secondary school of 1000 young people the incidence of mental illness can be expected to be as follows:

- 3 girls with anorexia nervosa

- 1 boy with anorexia nervosa (every three years)

- 50 young people with significant depressive disorder

- 5 young people with early onset psychosis

- 10 young people with obsessive compulsive disorder

- 40 with anxiety disorders.

Most emotional and behavioural problems in children and young people present in primary care to health visitors, school nurses, school teachers, general practitioners and community paediatricians. Only the more severe problems are referred to Child and Adolescent Mental Health Services (CAMHS).

Early intervention in psychosis is currently a government target as is a reduction in the suicide rate in young people. There is also an emphasis from the Department of Health on the prevention of anti-social behaviour, teenage pregnancy and drug and alcohol abuse in young people. The CAMHS have a role to play in all these areas.

Classification systems in psychiatry

There are two main classification systems of psychiatric illness: the International Classification of Diseases 10[3] (ICD-10), which is commonly used in Europe, and the Diagnostic and Statistical Manual of Mental Disorders IV[4] (DSM-IV), which is used in the USA, Canada, Australia and also in Europe. These classification systems are the result of a global consensus on how the diagnoses should be defined. DSM-IV includes additional information on the causes of mental illness, statistics in terms of gender, age at onset and

2   British Medical Association (2006) *Child and Adolescent Mental Health: A Guide for Health Care Professionals*, www.bma.org.uk (accessed 18.12.07).

3   World Health Organization (1992) *The ICD-10 Classification of Mental and Behavioural Disorders: Clinical Descriptions and Diagnostic Guidelines*. Geneva: WHO.

4   American Psychiatric Association (2005) *Diagnostic and Statistical Manual of Mental Disorders*, 4th edn. Washington, DC: American Psychiatric Association.

prognosis as well as some research concerning the optimal treatment approaches. These classification systems are revised regularly.

Both the classification systems are multi-axial and so, in addition to the diagnosis of mental illness, several other assessments about the person can be recorded.

In ICD-10 there are six axes:

- Axis 1: Clinical psychiatric syndrome
- Axis 2: Specific disorders of psychological development
- Axis 3: Intellectual level
- Axis 4: Medical conditions
- Axis 5: Associated abnormal psychosocial situations
- Axis 6: Global assessment of psychosocial disability.[5]

A system of classification is essential in order to communicate with mental health professionals in a meaningful way, gather information about incidence and prognosis, to proceed with research and to measure the effect of treatment interventions. Such categories therefore carry implications for the course of the illness, its prognosis and treatment.

When considering classification of mental illness in children, it has to be remembered that children are still developing, and therefore changing, so that any classification system must be able to take these changes into account and provide information in a developmental context. For example, a child of six, worried her mother will die in a car accident, might develop compulsive behaviours, such as counting up to ten, or avoiding cracks in the pavement, to prevent the dreaded outcome. Whilst this magical thinking is normal for a child of six it might be pathological in a teenager but less so if the teenager has learning difficulties.

There are several problems inherent in the classification of mental illness in children because it depends on observations of patterns of symptoms, which may include expressions of distress or behaviours, experienced to a degree by the whole population. There are no objective measures, such as abnormal blood tests, to confirm the presence of a psychiatric abnormality. Decisions about the cut-off point in order to fulfil specified criteria will remain subjective even with the help of standardised questionnaires.

---

5   World Health Organization (1996) *Multiaxial Classification of Child and Adolescent Psychiatric Disorders.* Cambridge: Cambridge University Press.

Diagnoses, labels and stigma

There is a social stigma attached to diagnoses of mental illness. Some argue that the use of diagnoses of mental illness in young people is potentially harmful because young people become labelled and at risk of permanent prejudice. The notion of deviance from the 'normal' inherent in categorical, as opposed to dimensional, systems of diagnosis may lead the young person to have an altered view of themselves which may aggravate problems and diminish self-worth. A diagnosis of mental illness can alter the way others react to the person and may have an impact on what is expected of that person. Teachers may adjust their expectations of an able pupil who has recently been diagnosed with psychosis. The use of categorical diagnoses may obscure individual differences and hinder a more detailed understanding of the mental function or the child's predicament.

If diagnosis is to be justified, its clinical value must be demonstrated. It should improve therapeutic responses, clarify thinking about the young person's condition and facilitate the delivery of services. For example, a diagnosis of attention deficit hyperactivity disorder (ADHD) may be received with relief by the young person who has developed the idea that they are 'bad' and 'stupid' on account of the reactions of parents and teachers to their challenging behaviour. The diagnosis, in this case, provides a better understanding and a more constructive way of managing the young person's difficulties. The diagnosis can help in correcting misperceptions and inappropriate labelling already associated with the young person who appears to be deliberately misbehaving in class.

Treatment

The reason for the admission of a young person with mental illness to psychiatric hospital is that the problem cannot be managed in any other way. Therefore, the decision will be determined, in part, by the resources of the family as well as those of community services in health, education and social services.

The hospital environment, maintained by 24-hour nursing care, is therapeutic in itself. Young patients benefit from the structure and routine of a well-run service, where they can rest from the chaos of their current predica-

---

6   Thornicroft, G., Rose, D., Kassam, A. and Sartorius, N. (2007) 'Stigma: ignorance, prejudice or discrimination?' *The British Journal of Psychiatry 190*, pages 192–193.

ment and acquire some space from the intense emotions of family relationships. A recent study of in-patient care for 8- to 18-year-olds suggested that these hospitals are effective for the group of young people with a very severe level of disorder, complexity and functional impairment.[7] Such benefits of admission come with some potential problems. There are risks, including the young person developing dependency on the hospital environment, members of staff disempowering parents in their care of the young person and the emergence of unhelpful interactions developing between the young person and members of staff, similar to well-established, but maladaptive, patterns of relating in the family. These risks can be reduced by open discussion with young people about the likely impact of hospital care, careful attention to the aims of admission, maintaining the involvement of parents through weekend leave arrangements and joint planning for discharge with the community team at an early stage.

In-patient settings should be age appropriate and offer suitable cultural, educational and recreational activities.[8] In-patient units offer multifaceted interventions by highly skilled staff including individual psychotherapy, particularly cognitive behavioural therapy, family therapy, group therapy and medication.

There has been considerable controversy about prescribing medication to young people, particularly with regard to the prescription of antidepressants in the form of specific serotonin reuptake inhibitors (SSRIs).[9] However, most young people requiring support at Tier 4 level will benefit from consideration of medication in the form of antidepressants, especially SSRIs, antipsychotics and antimanic preparations. The risk–benefit ratio must be carefully considered in each case, in the knowledge that in many circumstances current guidance has a relatively weak evidence base, because so little research has been completed in the adolescent population.[10] Although limited, the evidence for medication in the treatment of obsessive compulsive disorder (OCD), ADHD and psychosis in young people is compelling.

7   Jacob, B., Green, J., Kroll, L. *et al.* (2004) *Two and a Half Thousand Hours: The Children and Young Persons Inpatient Evaluation Study (CHYPIE) into Process and Outcome of Inpatient Child and Adolescent Psychiatric Care.* London: DH.
8   The Royal College of Psychiatrists has published guidance on the capacity and provision of specialist CAMHS. *Building and Sustaining Specialist Child and Adolescent Mental Health Services* (2006). Council Report CR 137. London: Royal College of Psychiatrists.
9   Jureidini, J.N., Doecke, J. *et al.* (2004) 'Efficacy and safety of anti-depressants for children and adolescents.' *British Medical Journal 328*, pages 879–883.
10   McArdle, P. (2007) 'Comments on NICE "Guidelines for Depression in Children and Young People".' *Child and Adolescent Mental Health 12*, 2, pages 66–69.

ECT is rarely administered to young people in the United Kingdom.[11] The indications for its use are the same as for adults: severe depression unresponsive to other treatments or complicated by life threatening self-neglect, when it can be life saving. Concerns about the effect of ECT on the developing neurological systems of younger patients have led to great caution in its use. The Mental Health Act 2007 introduces a requirement for the approval of a second opinion appointed doctor for ECT treatment to any patient under 18 years of age, regardless of whether or not the patient consents or is detained under the Act. (See Chapter 7.)

3 – The complex picture of mental illness in young people who present to Tier 4 services

Introduction

Children and young people who are experiencing difficulties severe enough to require psychiatric in-patient treatment and/or assessment under the Mental Health Act 1983 are likely to have diagnoses complicated by psychosocial factors and influenced significantly by family relationships and events. Some of the diagnoses applied to children and young people at this level, and the problems they face, are described below. Approaches to the care and treatment of these children and young people, and the management of their cases, are best illustrated by way of case examples. This narrative should therefore be used to highlight the various cases that follow.

Depressive disorder

For a diagnosis of depressive disorder in adults, according to ICD-10 criteria, core symptoms of low mood, lack of energy and lack of enjoyment are required with two or more symptoms of sleep disturbance, appetite disturbance, poor concentration, low self-esteem, ideas of guilt and worthlessness and profound pessimism. However, there are problems with the use of a system based on adult criteria because:

- young people find it more difficult to talk about emotions and give accurate historical data

---

11   Duffett, R., Hill, P. and Lelliot, P. (1999) 'Use of electroconvulsive therapy in young people.' *The British Journal of Psychiatry 175*, pages 228–230.

- sleep disturbance in young people may be excessive sleepiness rather than the typical sleep disturbance of depression in adults

- young people may have excessive rather than diminished appetite.

Additional manifestations of depression, not described in ICD-10, are more typical of depression in young people:

- running away from home

- separation anxiety (may present as school refusal)

- unexplained aches and pains

- decline in school work

- antisocial behaviour (mainly in boys)

- weight loss which may be masked by continuing growth.

Complaints of 'boredom' and 'poor memory' (actually poor concentration) are common. Young people may initially present with substance abuse, which represents an attempt to resolve symptoms by self-medication.

Up to 20 per cent of children in secondary schools are depressed.[12] Depressed children tend to come from families with high rates of psychopathology and may have experienced recent adverse life events including maltreatment.[13] Studies suggest that depressed children are at increased risk of depression in adulthood. Depressed children usually have multiple problems, such as educational failure, impaired psychosocial functioning and additional psychiatric disorders.[14]

Hearing voices

One of the tasks of a psychiatrist is to determine the diagnostic significance of the perceptual experience of the patient. Many young people who present to Tier 4 services complain of hearing voices. When the young person describes voices arising in external space (i.e. heard as noises arising outside

12   Costello, E.J., Mustillo, S., Erkanli, A. *et al.* (2003) 'Prevalence and development of psychiatric disorders in childhood and adolescence.' *Archives of General Psychiatry 60*, 8, pages 837–844.

13   Goodyer, I.M., Cooper, P.J., Vize, C. *et al.* (1993) 'Depression in 11 to 16 year old girls: the role of past parental psychopathology and exposure to recent life events.' *Journal of Child Psychology and Psychiatry 34*, pages 1103–1115.

14   Harrington, R.C. (2002) 'Affective Disorders.' In M. Rutter and E. Taylor (eds) *Child and Adolescent Psychiatry*, 3rd edn. Oxford: Blackwell.

the head rather than from inside the mind), the experience is known as auditory hallucinations and is characteristic of psychotic illness such as schizophrenia. Pseudo-auditory hallucinations (voices which seem to be arising in the mind, not in external space, and therefore not truly hallucinatory) occur in several other disorders such as post-traumatic stress disorder, emerging personality disorders, substance misuse, conduct disorders and Asperger's syndrome. Therefore, the experience of hearing voices in young people may not necessarily indicate a psychotic illness.

Young people who have been sexually abused often describe hearing voices of the perpetrator shouting at them in a derogatory manner and directing them to hurt or kill themselves. It is easier for the young person to manage these experiences, and diminish their impact, if the reasons for their occurrence are understood and worked through.

Child sexual abuse

Child sexual abuse is any sexual contact between an adult and a child who is sexually immature and unable to consent because of age or power differentials in the relationship.

Child sexual abuse

- This may occur by force, threat or deceit to gain the child's participation.

- Severity depends on the degree of threat, coercion, betrayal or intrusion and the chronicity and longer-term complications.

- The abuser is usually male and a member of the household, though not always.

- The child is trapped in a harmful pact, too fearful to disclose for fear of the potential consequences to themselves, the perpetrator or the whole family.

- The distress of the child may be expressed by way of a number of non-specific psychiatric symptoms.

For some young people, depressive disorder may develop subsequent to unresolved trauma of abuse. The young person may be unable for various reasons to disclose the abuse, making accurate diagnosis difficult. There is often a marked deterioration in a young person's coping mechanisms at the time of disclosure, and admission to hospital may provide a safe place, a sense of containment and separation from family, which all facilitate disclosure.

Deciding whether or not hospital admission is the best way forward for a young person with chronic low mood and self-harm in the context of probable but undisclosed past abuse can be very difficult. Sometimes admission can result in disclosure and the development of more constructive ways of coping. Sometimes the young person is not ready to disclose but wants to maintain care in hospital and dependency on staff for safety. Disclosing sexual abuse will have significant consequences for the young person and attempts to lead, rush or coerce such a disclosure should be resisted. At the same time, the limits and hazards associated with hospital admission must be given equal consideration.

Post-traumatic stress disorder

Post-traumatic stress disorder (PTSD)[15] describes a group of symptoms including: disturbing and recurrent recollections of trauma (flashbacks), avoidance of stimuli associated with the trauma, and increased physiological arousal. Flashbacks may present like psychotic symptoms, such as hallucinations, illusions or perceptual abnormalities. PTSD is most commonly seen in children following abuse, traffic accidents or life threatening illness. Young people often avoid discussing their experiences with their parents so as to minimise their own and their parents' distress. The more the parents are able to discuss the event and demonstrate effective coping strategies, the better the child's recovery.

If the PTSD is long standing, the young person may develop an ability to separate their emotional experience from what is, or has been, done to them. This ability to cut themselves off from the memories, experiences and emotions of traumatic experience is known as dissociation. The young person seems detached and, in the absence of a disclosure, it can be difficult to assess such people with any diagnostic certainty.

---

15   Yule, W. (1999) 'Post-traumatic stress disorder.' *Archives of Disease in Childhood 80*, pages 107–109.

Case 1

Summary
Following an initial diagnosis of depressive disorder, Claire's symptoms change and are better understood as PTSD following her disclosure of past intra-familial sexual abuse.

Claire (14) has been low in mood, withdrawn in her bedroom, refusing to eat and losing weight for months. She seems preoccupied by death and has taken three overdoses in addition to frequent superficial cutting of her arms. She is admitted to hospital with her mother's consent because of high risk of suicide. She is thought to be severely depressed.

What can Claire do if she does not agree with the decision about her care?

Two months later during psychotherapeutic work, Claire's mental state deteriorates. She is distressed, cannot sleep and is troubled by voices which tell her she is worthless and that she should kill herself. Claire wants to leave the hospital in order to end her life and makes several attempts to get past doors that are locked to keep her safe. She discloses intra-familial sexual abuse by her grandfather from the age of nine. She is terrified about the consequences of her disclosure on her family.

What would be the arguments for and against continuing Claire's in-patient treatment on the basis of the consent of her mother?

In order to manage her safety, Claire is treated in the intensive care area of the psychiatric hospital. She is highly agitated, unable to sleep and troubled by vivid flashbacks which result in her attempting to harm herself and run out of the unit. She refuses medication.

Given the change in Claire's behaviour how can her legal rights be best protected? Does changing her legal status conflict in any way with providing the psychiatric treatment that she needs?

Self-harm

Self-harm among young people is a major public health issue affecting one in every fifteen young people. Current figures suggest that numbers in the United Kingdom are the highest in Europe.[16]

Self-cutting with sharp implements, such as glass, broken CDs or razor blades, on the forearms and legs is often used as a coping mechanism for emotional pain or distress which cannot be otherwise communicated. Young people describe cutting as a way to express anger, relieve tension and punish themselves. Self-harm is often the outcome of a build-up of stressors in a person with poor coping resources and low resilience. Females are four times more likely to self-harm than males. The most common method in referred cases to hospital is by overdose of medication.

Young people can differentiate self-harm from suicidal behaviour. Suicidal behaviour is related to complex factors and is rarely a response to a single precipitant.[17] However, there is a strong association between attempted suicide, deliberate self-harm and subsequent successful suicide. One per cent of people who attempt suicide go on to succeed within a year of the attempt. Follow-up studies of teenagers show that 11 per cent will subsequently complete suicide.

Current clinical guidance from the National Institute for Health and Clinical Excellence recommends that every young person who self-harms should be assessed by a professional with knowledge and skills in mental health disorders in young people. However, not all self-harm is associated with a severe psychiatric disorder requiring psychiatric hospital admission.[18] Decisions concerning further treatment should be based on a comprehensive psychiatric, psychological, social and risk assessment.

16   Brophy, M. (2006) *Truth Hurts.:Report of the National Inquiry into Self-harm among Young People.* London: Mental Health Foundation, www.selfharmuk.org (accessed 19.12.07).
17   Hawton, K. (1996) 'Suicide and Attempted Suicide in Young People.' In A. McFarlane (ed.) *Adolescent Medicine.* London: Royal College of Physicians.
18   National Institute for Health and Clinical Excellence (2004) *Self-harm. Clinical Guideline 16:* www.nice.org.uk (accessed 19.12.07).

Borderline personality disorder

The ICD-10 diagnosis of emotionally unstable personality disorder, border-line type,[19] is described as a disorder in which there is a marked tendency to act impulsively without consideration of the consequences, together with instability of mood. The person may experience difficulty planning ahead. Outbursts of intense anger may lead to violence, which may be self-directed. The central themes are impulsiveness and lack of control. In addition, the subcategory 'borderline' implies that the person has a very poorly developed sense of their own identity and experiences chronic feelings of emptiness. Relationships with others are disrupted by intense attachments or fear of abandonment which may be acted out in threats of self-harm or suicide. Such manifestations appear during childhood or adolescence and continue into adulthood. The abnormal behaviour is enduring and not limited to episodes of mental illness, though such individuals are more at risk of developing mental illness, particularly depression and harmful use of alcohol. Though the characteristic behaviours emerge during adolescence, there is reluctance to make such a diagnosis in a young person who has scope for improvement with age. Promising developments in treatment have begun to diminish the stigma associated with the diagnosis.

Case 2

Summary
Tanya frequently self-harms and threatens suicide in the context of long-standing grossly dysfunctional family relationships which have had a significant impact on her personality development.

Tanya (14) has cut herself with razors for years. Her parents separated soon after her birth and mother has had several partners, none of whom have provided stable care for Tanya. There has been a background of domestic violence and Tanya's mother had episodes of depression. More recently, Tanya's attendance at school has deteriorated; she is abusive to teachers, running away from home and is frequently under the influence of alcohol and illicit drugs. Tanya has a violent temper and frequently damages property in her home. Tanya's mother requested the support of social services because she feels she can no longer cope.

---

19   World Health Organization (1996) *Disorders of Adult Personality and Behaviour: Multiaxial Classification of Child and Adolescent Psychiatric Disorders.* Cambridge: Cambridge University Press.

*What would be the grounds (if any) in this case to justify the local
authority in applying for a care order? What would be the purpose
of obtaining a care order?*

One day, Tanya was found cold and miserable, having consumed half
a bottle of vodka and paracetamol tablets. Following hospital
treatment for her overdose she was assessed under the Mental Health
Act 1983. The ASW decided that criteria for detention were not met
and a place was found in a social services residential unit for young
people with complex problems. Tanya ran away and phoned the
police on her mobile saying she was at the nearby car park about to
jump off. An application for a secure accommodation order under
section 25 of the Children Act 1989 was subsequently made.

*What are the grounds for making a secure accommodation order
under the Children Act? What would be the arguments for and
against a Mental Health Act assessment?*

Bipolar affective disorder

For a diagnosis of bipolar disorder (BPD), the ICD-10 diagnostic criteria[20]
stipulate at least two episodes of significantly disturbed mood and activity
with, on occasion, either mood elation and hyperactivity or depression with
decreased activity and energy. Symptoms should last at least one week and
severely disrupt normal functioning and include:

- carefree joviality to uncontrollable excitement

- over-activity with pressure of speech

- decreased need for sleep

- loss of inhibitions and concentration

- inflated self-esteem and over-optimistic ideas

- perceptual disorders, preoccupation with fine detail

- extravagant and impractical schemes

- amorousness.

Psychotic symptoms may develop if BPD is very severe and occur more
commonly in young people than adults. The peak onset of BPD is in the 15-
to 19-year-old group with a male to female ratio of 1:1. There is controversy

---

20   World Health Organization (1992) *Mood Disorders. The ICD-10 Classification of Mental and
     Behavioural Disorders: Clinical Descriptions and Diagnostic Guidelines.* Geneva: WHO.

about the prevalence of BPD in children, when it is often under-diagnosed.[21] Seventy per cent of those developing BPD present initially with severe depression and the diagnosis of BPD is made later, when symptoms of mania emerge. In the past, young people presenting with BPD and psychotic symptoms were misdiagnosed as having schizophrenia. There has since been greater recognition that psychotic illness is often poorly differentiated in young people and it is unwise to diagnose a specific psychotic illness with any certainty until adulthood.

Young people are more likely than adults with mania to present with a picture of irritability, mixed symptoms of mania and depression, and a rapid cycling pattern of mood disturbance. BPD in young people often occurs with ADHD, substance misuse and anxiety disorder. The course of the illness in young people is more prolonged and less responsive to treatment than in adults. The risk of suicide is greater than that for young people with depressive disorder.[22]

Case 3

Summary
Ben appears to be intoxicated and behaving dangerously. A family history of bipolar disorder suggests an alternative explanation.

Ben, a 15-year-old boy, is found by police climbing buildings and jumping from one to another. When approached he seems confused, talking rapidly and inconsequentially, claiming to have supernatural powers to read the policeman's thoughts. He becomes irritable and hostile when the policeman attempts to secure his safety. With the help of a colleague he is brought to the police station where his mother joins him for a psychiatric assessment under section 136 of Mental Health Act 1983. Ben's mother reports that he has been behaving oddly for weeks. There is no history of drug use, but a family history of bipolar disorder. In the absence of an in-patient adolescent psychiatric bed, a bed is found on the paediatric ward with the additional support of a mental health trained nurse. His mother argues for him to be admitted under her responsibility and once in the hospital, removes his shoes and clothes so that he cannot leave.

---

21   *Child and Adolescent Bipolar Disorder: An Update from the National Institute of Mental Health* (2000), www.nimh.nih.gov (accessed 19.12.07).

22   Geller, B. and Luby, J. (1997) 'Child and adolescent bipolar disorder: a review of the past ten years.' *Journal of the American Academy of Child and Adolescent Psychiatry 36*, pages 1168–1176.

What legal authority do the paediatric nursing team have to protect Ben should he try to leave the ward?

Obsessive compulsive disorder

For a diagnosis of obsessive compulsive disorder according to ICD-10[23] there must be obsessions (thoughts) or compulsions (acts) or both on most days for a period of at least two weeks associated with distress and interference with normal functioning. The majority of young people with OCD have both obsessions and compulsions, such as checking, washing and straightening until things seem just right. OCD in young people is associated with tics and Tourette's syndrome. The course is often chronic in young people with a complete recovery rate of only 15 per cent.[24]

Case 4

Summary
Brian and his family have been struggling for years to manage his severe OCD. Even though Brian is dangerously ill his parents do not want to be separated from him by hospital admission.

Brian, aged 15, is obsessed with studying. He spends hours rehearsing equations and formulae in his head. The obsession has taken over his life. He no longer meets friends or enjoys hobbies or sports. He has withdrawn into his bedroom, is missing meals, losing weight and sleeping little. His family cannot stop the process. He is low in mood and hopeless about his situation. A Mental Health Act assessment is requested because Brian's mother can no longer manage him at home but she and her husband have significant doubts about the proposed plan for in-patient treatment. Following assessment, he is brought into hospital under section 2 of the Mental Health Act 1983 with the assistance of ambulance crew and the police.

What rights do Brian's mother and father have under the Mental Health Act in relation to the assessment, admission and treatment of their son?

---

23   World Health Organization (1992) *Neurotic, Stress-related and Somatoform Disorders. The ICD-10 Classification of Mental and Behavioural Disorders: Clinical Descriptions and Diagnostic Guidelines.* Geneva: WHO.

24   Shafran, R. (2001) 'Obsessive compulsive disorder in children and adolescents.' *Child Psychology and Psychiatry Review*, 6, 2.

Anorexia nervosa

Anorexia remains the psychiatric disorder with the highest mortality. In early onset, anorexia nervosa mortality rates of up to 18 per cent have been reported in the literature.[25] Death results from starvation and suicide and occurs in the first eight years. Mortality rates are similar to those reported for adult patients. Although there are increasing numbers of specialist oupatient

---

Anorexia nervosa

For a diagnosis of anorexia nervosa according to ICD-10[26] all the following problems must be present:

- Body weight is maintained at least 15 per cent below that expected, or Body Mass Index 17.5 or less. Pre-pubertal patients may show failure to make the expected weight gain during period of growth.

- The weight loss is self-induced by avoiding fatty foods. One or more of the following must be present: self-induced vomiting, self-induced purging, excessive exercise, use of appetite suppressants and/or diuretics.

- There is body image distortion in the form of a specific psychopathology whereby a dread of fatness persists as an intrusive, overvalued idea and the patient imposes a low weight threshold on herself/himself.

- A widespread endocrine disorder is manifest in women as amenorrhoea (periods stop) and in men as loss of sexual interest and potency. There may be other hormonal changes.

- If the onset is pre-pubertal the sequence of pubertal events is delayed or even arrested. Growth ceases. In girls the breasts do not develop and menstrual periods do not start; in boys genitals do not develop and remain juvenile. With recovery puberty is often complete and menarche is late.

---

25 Lask, B. and Bryant-Waugh, R. (2000) *Anorexia Nervosa and Related Eating Disorders in Childhood and Adolescence*, 2nd edn. Hove: Psychology Press.

26 World Health Organization (1992) *The ICD-10 Classification of Mental and Behavioural Disorders: Clinical Descriptions and Diagnostic Guidelines*. Geneva: WHO.

services in the country for the younger age group with eating disorders, in-patient treatment in a unit with expertise in managing eating disorders may be required, particularly if there is extreme weight loss, suicidal risk or lack of progress in the community. Urgent medical care in a general hospital may be necessary if there are physical complications such as dehydration, biochemical abnormalities or cardiac complications.

The management of eating disorder in young people requires effective collaboration with families because the nature of the disorder gives rise to conflict between those trying to help the young person. This often leads to deliberations about how far to work with the consent of the young person and their parent/s and at what stage to consider the use of the Mental Health Act 1983. This can require considerable skill in negotiation and motivational work.

The outlook is variable and recovery often takes years. The majority of young people who have required hospital treatment continue to have problems eating, mood disorders and personality difficulties. Whether or not hospital admission aggravates the chronicity of the disorder is a controversial issue;[27] however, there are occasions when admission to a service with specialist skills is necessary to prevent further deterioration which might lead to death from dehydration, starvation and suicide.

Case 5

Summary
Gill has severe anorexia nervosa and her treatment is complicated by her family's denial of her disorder.

Gill, aged 15, had been admitted to an adolescent in-patient unit with the consent of her parents because of her extremely low weight, secondary to severe anorexia nervosa. Although she did not agree to her treatment and care plan she did not resist any of the treatment interventions and accepted a short period of nasogastric feeding, with the consent of her parents, in the early stages of her treatment. As she progressed her parents began to question the treatment, arguing that the estimated healthy weight was too high and that they thought their daughter healthy despite the fact that her periods had ceased for 18 months and a bone scan showed very thin bones.

---

27   Gowers, S.G. *et al.* (2000) 'Impact of hospitalization on the outcome of adolescent anorexia nervosa.' *The British Journal of Psychiatry 176*, pages 138–141.

What would be the arguments against nasogastric feeding a non-consenting young person with parental authority?

Gill's treatment depended to a degree on teaching her parents how to encourage eating at home. The parents were unable to take charge of their daughter's meals and allowed her to miss meals and reduce the portion size. They also encouraged her to join them at the local athletics club every weekend to compete. Gill's progress on the unit faltered and she began losing weight as her parents requested increasing periods of home leave.

How would you decide if Gill is competent to make decisions about her treatment on the unit?

Early onset psychosis

The term 'psychosis' is used when mental illness causes the person to behave in such a bizarre and inappropriate manner that he or she appears to have lost touch with reality. The symptoms of psychotic illnesses include the experience of delusions, hallucinations, disorganised thoughts and speech, grossly disorganised behaviour as well as social dysfunction. Psychotic illnesses comprise a large group of more specific diagnoses, for example schizophrenia, persistent delusional disorder and schizoaffective disorder. As these specific diagnoses are based on patterns of symptom and behaviour in adults, the categories are not easily applicable to children and young people.

It can be difficult to be certain of the diagnosis of a specific psychotic illness in adolescence. The picture often changes with time and can be very mixed with overlap in symptom patterns. However, there is often urgency to diagnose and begin effective treatment because of evidence that the longer the untreated phase of illness, the worse the prognosis.[28] For this reason it is standard practice to refer to 'early onset psychosis' and to leave the diagnosis undifferentiated for several years unless the criteria for one of the specific psychotic disorders, such as schizophrenia, are absolutely and exclusively fulfilled. As described previously, psychotic symptoms can occur with mood disorders such as depressive disorder and bipolar disorder.[29]

---

28   Johnstone, E.C., Crow, T.J., Johnson, A.L. *et al.* (1986) 'The Northwich Park Study of first episodes of schizophrenia. 1. Presentation of the illness and problems relating to admission.' *The British Journal of Psychiatry 148*, pages 115–120.

29   Turner, T.H. (2004) 'Long-term outcome of treating schizophrenia.' *British Medical Journal 329*, pages 1058–1059.

Psychiatric treatment in hospital may be necessary for young people with psychotic illnesses. Reasons for hospital treatment include failure to respond to medication, the family being unable to cope or if there is a significant risk to the young person, the family or others. Psychoses account for the highest rates of hospital admission of young people to adult wards. The availability of early onset intervention teams, which have the ability to provide more intensive support to the young patient and his family in his home, may reduce the need for hospital admission.

The average CAMHS with a total population of 150,000 will have approximately 19 young people with a diagnosis of psychosis. Almost half of this number will eventually fulfil the diagnostic criteria for schizophrenia.[30]

Case 6

Summary
Lee has developed early onset psychosis following heavy use of cannabis and, despite his abstinence from cannabis, he remains troubled by psychotic symptoms.

Lee (15) dropped out of school and spent his time smoking cannabis with a group of older boys who were involved in petty crime. One evening he returned home battered and bruised following a fight and seemed very paranoid and aggressive. He accused his mother of trying to steal his money and threatened her with a knife. Following police involvement and a psychiatric assessment, he was admitted to the local adult psychiatric ward under section 2 of the Mental Health Act 1983.

Can Lee apply to a Mental Health Review Tribunal?

Twenty-eight days later Lee remained paranoid. He thought that he was being watched constantly by satellite and that he would be attacked by special agents. He described hearing voices in his room at night which talked about him and laughed about what would be done to him. He thought he received messages from the TV that he would be executed and was convinced the nurses could read his

---

30   Hayes, D. (2001) *Department of Health Early Intervention Working Group: Early Onset Psychosis, Childhood and Adolescence.*

mind. His urine screens for cannabis were now negative. He accepted anti-psychotic medication and was generally cooperative on the unit.

Would it be justified to place Lee on a section 3 treatment order at the expiry of the section 2 order?

Autism

People with autism have difficulties in three key areas: social interaction, communication and interests which are restricted and repetitive. Problems arise because of obsessional interests, rituals and fixed behaviours, and unusual sensory interests, such as a compulsion to lick everything. Typically young people cope badly with changes in their routine and dislike change generally.

The symptoms and signs which lead to a diagnosis of autism exist on a continuum so that there is enormous variation among young people on the autistic spectrum. These differences can be explained by the intelligence of the young person, their language development, their age, sociability and temperament. Two-thirds of children with autism have learning difficulties, though young people with Asperger's syndrome may have above-average intelligence. Young people with autistic spectrum disorders frequently have other diagnoses, particularly anxiety disorders, depression, obsessive compulsive disorder, psychosis and attention deficit hyperactivity disorder.

Asperger's syndrome

The term 'Asperger's syndrome' is used when there are problems in social interaction, communication and interests but early language development appears normal in contrast to autism where there is a delay in language development. Though speech has developed at a normal rate, and may be correct in terms of grammar and vocabulary, it may seem professor-like, stilted and pedantic with little reciprocity. Many young people with Asperger's syndrome want to be sociable but do not understand the unspoken rules of social engagement, thereby appearing odd or strange and easy targets for bullying. Often young people with Asperger's syndrome are exceptionally knowledgeable about certain topics, such as timetables, maps or astronomy.[31]

Young people with high-functioning autism or Asperger's syndrome sometimes develop secondary psychiatric illness when the extra demands of adolescence, both academic and social, cause a sudden deterioration in their ability to function in society. Energy spent reviewing educational needs and finding more appropriate educational placements may usefully avoid the need for psychiatric hospital admission. Admitting a young person with autism to an in-patient psychiatric hospital can cause a great deal of distress on account of their difficulty coping with change and making new acquaintances.

Case 7

Summary
Jim is hospitalised because of depression and suicidal risk, but it becomes clear that he has problems associated with previously unidentified autism and this leads to recommendations for consideration of specialist educational services.

Jim refused to attend school following his 16th birthday. He had specific learning difficulties and the transition to upper school from middle school resulted in a spate of bullying. He became very low in mood and started to self-harm by cutting his wrists with a knife. Jim had difficulty socialising, problems communicating and an obsessional interest in trains to the exclusion of all other interests. Jim's behaviour deteriorated and he tried to drown himself by swimming out to sea, resulting in a request for in-patient admission and a full review of his educational needs.

Would the Mental Capacity Act assist in enabling and supporting Jim?

Conclusions

In the last ten years community mental health services for young people have made significant developments, yet there remain many occasions when

31   Attwood, T. (1997) *Asperger's Syndrome: A Guide for Parents and Professionals.* London: Jessica Kingsley Publishers.

hospital admission is the only safe way forward for a young person in crisis. When a decision is made to admit a young person to a psychiatric hospital it must be made with careful regard to the rights of the young person and within established legal frameworks. Such decisions require a sophisticated understanding of psychiatric illness in young patients together with the potential risks associated with hospitalisation. It is important that psychiatric in-patient services are available for young people when they need them and that admission brings more benefits than problems. High-quality, evidence-based standards for in-patient units for young people have been established and are regularly audited by the Quality Network for In-patient CAMHS.[32]

---

32   *QNIC Service Standards 2005 / 6* (Quality Network for In-patient CAMHS), Royal College of Psychiatrists, College Research Unit.

Part 3

Problem Areas

Chapter 11

Confidentiality

Introduction

Working with, and treating, children and young people requires an understanding of their entitlement to confidentiality.

> All children and young people have a right to confidentiality. Gillick competent under 16s and young people aged 16 or 17 are entitled to make decisions about the use and disclosure of information they have provided in confidence in the same way as adults, e.g. they may be receiving treatment or counselling about which they do not want their parents to know.[1]

Where there has been a dispute about the disclosure of information the courts have regarded guidance from both professional bodies and central government as being of particular importance and therefore this chapter covers the law and current guidance. The first part of the chapter covers some of the principles of the law of confidentiality. The second part outlines some of the provisions of the Data Protection Act 1998 which imposes duties on organisations to regulate the circumstances in which data may be 'processed'; this term includes obtaining, holding, using or disclosing information. The third part identifies some of the circumstances when an individual's entitlement to confidentiality might be qualified or limited. The fourth part discusses some aspects of the law of confidentiality as it applies to children and young people.

---

1 Department of Health (2007) *Mental Health Act 1983 Draft revised Code of Practice*. London: DH, paragraph 39.55.

1 – The law of confidentiality

The common law principles in relation to the duty of confidence can be simply stated:

> A duty of confidence arises when confidential information comes to the knowledge of a person (the confidant) in circumstances where he has notice, or is held to have agreed, that the information is confidential, with the effect that it would be just in all the circumstances that he should be precluded from disclosing the information to others.[2]

The relationship between health professional and patient constitutes such a circumstance. In the event, therefore, of breach of this duty, legal action may follow including injunction and damages. Although this relationship creates an obligation of confidence the patient can, by consenting to the disclosure of information, waive that obligation.

The public interest argument for confidentiality, even for a child who is not competent to make a fully informed decision on confidentiality issues, is that unless children feel able to trust the professional to keep information secret they will not be candid about revealing it.[3] The child or young person therefore has a 'right' to confidentiality; this right can be qualified, or limited, in a number of different circumstances.

Where there is a dispute about disclosure of confidential information it is likely that Article 8 (ECHR) will apply. This means that any decision concerning the disclosure of confidential information about a child or young person without their consent requires an analysis of whether the decision to disclose is 'proportionate', that is 'whether the proposed sharing [of information] is a proportionate response to the need to protect the public interest in question'.[4]

2 – The Data Protection Act 1998

The Data Protection Act 1998 (DPA) is intended to implement the 1995 Data Protection Directive. It governs the use ('processing' in the language of

---

2   *A-G* v. *Guardian (No 2)* [1988] 3 All ER 545.
3   Montgomery, J. (2003) *Health Care Law*, 2nd edn. Oxford: Oxford University Press, page 309.
4   Department for Educational Skills (2006) *Information Sharing: Practitioners' Guide*. London: DFES, paragraph 3.10, www.everychildmatters.gov.uk/informationsharing (accessed 18.12.07).

the Act) of 'personal data', which means information about a living individual who can be identified from the data.

Data protection principles

At the core of the Data Protection Act 1998 are the eight principles of Schedule 1, created under the 1995 Directive. These are:

First Principle: Personal data shall be processed fairly and lawfully, and in particular shall not be processed unless (a) at least one of the conditions in Schedule 2 is met, and (b) in the case of sensitive personal data, at least one of the conditions in Schedule 3 is also met. (See below.) 'Processing' includes recording, disclosing and deleting of data.

Second Principle. Personal data shall be obtained only for one or more specified and lawful purposes and shall not be further processed in any manner incompatible with that purpose or those purposes.

Third Principle: Personal data shall be adequate, relevant and not excessive in relation to the purpose or purposes for which they are processed.

Fourth Principle: Personal data shall be accurate and, where necessary, kept up to date.

Fifth Principle: Personal data kept for any purpose or purposes shall not be kept for longer than is necessary for that purpose or those purposes.

Sixth Principle: Personal data shall be processed in accordance with the rights of data subjects under the Act.

Seventh Principle: Appropriate technical and organisational measures shall be taken against unauthorised or unlawful processing of personal data and against accidental loss or destruction of, or damage to, personal data.

Eighth Principle: Personal data shall not be transferred to a country outside the European Economic Area unless that country provides adequate protection for the rights of data subjects with regard to processing of data.

Processing personal data under the Data Protection Act 1998

General data may only be processed if one of the conditions set out in Schedule 2 of the Data Protection Act 1998 is met. The most important is that the 'data subject' has given his or her consent to disclosure or other processing.

Special rules apply to the processing of 'sensitive personal data', including health records, sexual history, the commission (or alleged commission) of offences, ethnicity, political views and so on. Here, one of the circumstances in Schedule 3 must also apply. These are tighter than Schedule 2, for example consent must be expressed not implied. Under Schedule 3, circumstances where data can be shared without consent include: to protect the vital interests of the data subject or another person, in connection with any legal proceedings, for the administration of justice and where it is 'necessary for medical purposes'. 'In connection with legal proceedings' would cover, for example, a doctor or health professional being required to attend court to give evidence in Children Act proceedings.

The Data Protection (Processing of Sensitive Personal Data) Order 2000[5] specifies various further circumstances in which the processing of certain categories of sensitive personal data will be lawful. These include processing without consent for the purposes of prevention or detection of any unlawful act.

Generally under the Data Protection Act 1998, disclosure without consent is only permitted where it is 'necessary'. In other words, before an unauthorised disclosure, the following should be considered: by obtaining consent, whether the same result can be achieved without breaching confidentiality (for example, by anonymising the information) and minimising what can be disclosed. Although in certain circumstances the Act permits disclosure without consent, the Act does not require it. The person wishing to disclose information, having checked that it would be lawful, must then decide whether it is appropriate in all the circumstances.

There is no age limit in relation to the provision of consent in the DPA and so the principles contained in the Gillick case for those under 16, and the Mental Capacity Act 2005 for the 16- to 17-year-olds, will apply.

Accessing personal data under the Data Protection Act 1998

The Data Protection Act 1998 does not contain any age limits in relation to accessing data. Guidance published by the Information Commissioner under the heading 'subject access requests made on behalf of children' states that

---

5   SI 2000 No. 417.

by the age of 12 a child can be expected to have sufficient maturity to understand the nature of the request to access data and that a child may 'reach sufficient maturity earlier and it will be a question of fact in each case'. The
guidance continues:

> A data controller who receives a subject access request on behalf of a
> child will need to judge whether the child understands the nature of the
> request. If the child understands, he or she is entitled to exercise the
> right and the data controller should reply to the child.

> If the child does not understand the nature of the request, someone
> with parental responsibility for the child, or a guardian, is entitled to
> make the request on behalf of the child and to receive the response.[6]

Access to health, education and social work records is further regulated by
statutory instrument and access may be refused in certain specified circumstances, for example that disclosure 'would be likely to cause serious harm to
the physical or mental health or condition of the data subject or any other
person'.[7]

The interrelationship between the common law, the Data Protection Act and the Human Rights Act

The mother of a 27-year-old learning-disabled man (C) requested access
to specified information from his social services files. He lacked the
capacity to consent to her seeing them. At issue was how C's interests in
preserving the confidentiality of personal information about himself was
to be reconciled with his mother's interests, as his nearest relative, in
having access to enough information about him to exercise her statutory
functions under the Mental Health Act 1983.

---

6   Information Commissioner, *Data Protection Act 1998: Legal Guidance.* ICO, paragraph
     4.1.6.
7   Data Protection (Subject Access Modification) (Health) Order 2000 (SI 2000 No. 413),
     regulation 5(1). Similar provisions are contained in the Data Protection (Subject Access
     Modification) (Social Work) Order 2000 (SI 2000 No. 415) and the Data Protection
     (Subject Access Modification) (Education) Order 2000,(SI 2000 No. 414).

The court considered the Data Protection Act, the common law and the Human Rights Act.[8] The Data Protection Act did not provide much assistance. It was common ground that the Act did not prevent the local authority disclosing the information. Nor did it require the local authority to do so. The common law and the Human Rights Act required that the dilemma be resolved by striking a balance between the various interests involved. These were:

> The confidentiality of the information sought; the proper adminis-tration of justice; the mother's right of access to legal advice to enable her to decide whether or not to exercise a right which is likely to lead to legal proceedings against her if she does so; the rights of both C and his mother to respect for their family life and adequate involve-ment in decision-making processes about it; C's right to respect for his private life; and the protection of C's welfare.[9]

The balance in this case led to the disclosure of the relevant information from C's files to his mother.

In the course of the judgment Hale J added:

> C's interest in protecting the confidentiality of personal information about himself must not be underestimated. It is all too easy for profes-sionals and parents to regard children and incapacitated adults as having no independent interest of their own: as objects rather than subjects.[10]

3 – Limiting the right to confidentiality

Both statute and common law recognise circumstances in which the right to confidentiality may or must be qualified. These circumstances must now be read in conjunction with the DPA and orders made under it.

---

8   *The Queen on the application of S* v. *Plymouth City Council (C as interested party)* [2002] 1 FLR 1177.
9   Hale J, paragraph 48, page 1193.
10   Hale J, paragraph 49, page 1193.

Statute law

In addition to the DPA other statutes can modify and qualify the obligation of confidence. For example, the Public Health (Control of Diseases) Act 1984 requires a doctor to notify actual or suspected cases of patients suffering from various forms of infectious diseases to the local authority. Where the use of compulsion is being considered in respect of a person who is mentally disordered, the Mental Health Act 1983 qualifies the obligation of confidence by requiring that a patient's nearest relative must be consulted (but consider the discussion about the Bristol case in Chapter 9) before an application for admission under the Act is made.

Confidentiality and the Mental Health Act 1983

Section 11, which deals with the procedure for compulsory admission to hospital, sets down the following requirements. In the case of an application under section 2 (see Chapter 9), a social worker shall take such steps that are practicable to inform the person (if any) who appears to be the nearest relative that the application is to be or has been made and of the power of the nearest relative to order the patient's discharge, and in the case of an application for admission for treatment or guardianship no application may be made by a social worker unless there has been consultation with the nearest relative and that person does not object to the application being made.

Consultation need not take place if it appears to the social worker that, in the circumstances, such consultation is not reasonably practicable or would involve unreasonable delay.

Section 133 requires a hospital to notify the nearest relative of a detained patient's discharge, if practicable at least seven days before it is due to take place. However, if the patient (or the nearest relative) objects to this information being given, the duty does not apply, so any disclosure is subject to the rules on confidentiality discussed in this chapter. This section will also apply to patients on CTOs.

Under section 25B(3) of the Mental Health (Patients in the Community) Act 1995 the RMO is required to consult a patient's nearest relative before making a supervision application. The patient is entitled to object to this consultation. The RMO can consult regardless of the patient's

---

Disclosure is necessary for medical purposes – 'need to know'

A conventional view of medical practice assumes that there will be shared information within a medical team. For example, a patient who consults a doctor implicitly consents to the doctor disclosing such information about the patient to other staff to allow the doctor to treat the patient. Health service providers rely on this basic assumption in relation to the provision of modern health care.

Under the Data Protection Act 1998 health information may be processed without consent between health professionals or others who owe a similar duty of confidentiality. This condition will not permit disclosure of health information to a family member. Therefore, a communication made to one professional, for example a psychiatrist or psychotherapist, may be shared with a multi-disciplinary team, for example a social worker, nurse, psychologist and occupational therapist. Any wider sharing can of course be covered by the express consent of the person concerned.

Opportunities should be taken to check that patients understand and consent. Special attention should be paid to the issues around child consent.[11] 'You may share some limited information, with consent if possible, to decide if there is a risk that would justify further disclosures. A risk might only become apparent when a number of persons with niggling concerns share them.'[12]

Public interest

Where information sharing is not directly concerned with patient health care then explicit consent should be obtained. If however consent is refused, or cannot be obtained because to do so could place a child at risk, then information may be shared on the basis of a public interest justification. Although there is a tendency to apply the term loosely, the courts have been restrictive about its application.

> Rarely, disclosure may be justified on the ground that it is in the public interest which, in certain circumstances such as, for example, investigation by the police of a grave or very serious crime, might override the doctor's duty to maintain his patient's confidence.[13]

---

11   Department of Health (2003) *Confidentiality: NHS Code of Practice*. London: DH, paragraph 15.
12   General Medical Council (2007) *0–18 Years: Guidance for all Doctors*. London: GMC.
13   *W* v. *Egdell* [1990] 1 All ER 835.

Child protection

This area, more than any other, causes concerns for practitioners. It is well established that both the common law and the Data Protection Act 1998 allow disclosure in the public interest, and therefore where abuse is suspected then disclosure without consent may be justified on this basis.

Although arguments have been used to justify a general obligation to disclose confidential information where the best interests of the child require such disclosure, there is no legal basis for this suggestion. It is therefore necessary for professionals always to identify the public interest grounds that exist in each particular case where disclosure without consent is being contemplated. This position is reflected in current government guidance:

> In deciding whether there is a need to share information, professionals need to consider their legal obligations, including whether they have a duty of confidentiality to the child. Where there is such a duty, the professional may lawfully share information if the child consents or if there is a public interest of sufficient force. This must be judged by the professional on the facts of each case. Where there is a clear risk of significant harm to a child, or serious harm to adults, the public interest test will almost certainly be satisfied. However, there will be other cases where practitioners will be justified in sharing some confidential information in order to make decisions on sharing further information or taking action – the information shared should be proportionate.[14]

The Data Protection Act 1998 allows for the disclosure in certain conditions, without the consent of the data subject. These conditions include: for the purposes of the prevention or detection of crime, and in relation to the apprehension or prosecution of offenders where failure to disclose would be likely to prejudice those objectives in a particular case.

Practitioners unfamiliar with child protection processes are sometimes uncertain as to whom information should be disclosed. The Local Safeguarding Children Board provides the structure and guidance for inter-agency cooperation. Guidance on the disclosure of information to protect and safeguard children will be made available by the boards.[15] CAMHS

---

14   Department for Education and Skills (2006) *Working Together to Safeguard Children: A Guide to Inter-agency Working to Safeguard and Promote the Welfare of Children*. London: TSO, paragraph 5.21.

15   London Safeguarding Children Board have published *London Child Protection Procedure*, 3rd edn, 2007. See paragraph 5.35.6 for advice in relation to disclosure of information

professionals should follow the child protection procedures established for the services within their own areas.

Providing specific, rather than general, guidance about the extent, and amount of information to disclose about a particular child or young person is not possible. The core principles of the Data Protection Act 1998 must be applied. British Medical Association (BMA) guidance on public interest disclosure advises professionals to 'reveal only the minimum necessary to achieve the objective'.[16] In the context of developing a plan to protect a child the objectives of disclosure will vary. It may be to allow a full risk assessment to take place, or it may be simply to establish a psychiatric diagnosis and treatment plan. The information necessary to make a full risk assessment may itself have to be the subject of discussion with other child care professionals.

4 – Children, young people and the law of confidentiality

The Gillick-competent child and confidentiality

A particular principle from the case of *Gillick*,[17] followed and brought up to date in the case of *Axon*,[18] is that a medical professional need not notify a child's parents before giving advice or treatment on sexual matters to the child providing that the professional is satisfied as to the following matters:

(1) that the young person although under 16 years of age understands *all* aspects of the advice. In the light of Lord Scarman's comments in Gillick at 189C and 253 respectively set out in para (13) (v) above, he or she must 'have sufficient maturity to understand what is involved' that understanding includes all relevant matters and it is not limited to family and moral aspects as well as all possible adverse consequences which might follow from the advice;

(2) that the medical professional cannot persuade the young person to inform his or her parents or to allow the medical professional to inform the parents that their child is seeking advice and/or treatment on sexual matters. (As stated in the 2004 Guidance, where

about abuse or neglect made by children in psychiatric settings, www.londonscb.gov.uk (accessed 18.12.07).

16   *Medical Ethics Today: The BMA's Handbook of Ethics and Law* (2004), 2nd edn. London: BMA/BMJ Books, page 192.

17   *Gillick* v. *West Norfolk and Wisbech Area Health Authority and another* [1985] 3 All ER.

18   *R (Axon)* v. *The Secretary of State for Health and the Family Planning Association* [2006] 2 FLR 206.

the young person cannot be persuaded to involve a parent, every effort should be made to persuade the young person to help find another adult (such as another family member or a specialist youth worker) to provide support to the young person);

(3) that (in any case in which the issue is whether the medical professional should advise on or treat in respect of contraception and sexually transmissible illnesses) the young person is very likely to begin or to continue having sexual intercourse with or without contraceptive treatment or treatment for a sexually transmissible disease;

(4) that unless the young person receives advice and treatment on the relevant sexual matters, his or her physical or mental health or both are likely to suffer. (In considering this requirement, the medical professional must take into account all aspects of the young person's health); and

(5) that the best interests of the young person require him or her to receive advice and treatment on sexual matters without parental consent or notification.[19]

Competent children and young people with capacity

The *Gillick* and *Axon* cases do not provide authority for the proposition that a child has the same rights to confidentiality as an adult. The 'refusal' cases discussed in Chapter 12 make clear that whilst a competent under 16-year-old (or a 17- to 18-year-old with capacity) may have a right to choose treatment without external control, the refusal of the child or young person may be overridden by the court or person with parental responsibility. This distinction between consent and refusal is reflected in the law of confidentiality.

Recent government guidance on the law of confidentiality *Confidentiality: NHS Code of Practice*[20] supersedes previous guidance[21] on confidentiality. This code contains the following paragraphs in relation to children and young people:

---

19   *R (Axon)* v. *The Secretary of State for Health and the Family Planning Association* [2006] 2 FLR 206, paragraph 154.

20   Department of Health (2003) *Confidentiality: NHS Code of Practice.* London: DH.

21   Department of Health (1996) *Protection and Use of Patient Information.* HSG(96)18/LASSL(96)5. London: DH.

Young people aged 16 or 17 are presumed to be competent for the purposes of consent to treatment and are therefore entitled to the same duty of confidentiality as adults. Children under the age of 16 who have the capacity and understanding to take decisions about their own treatment are also entitled to make decisions about the use and disclosure of information they have provided in confidence (e.g. they may be receiving treatment or counselling about which they do not want their parents to know).

However, where a competent young person or child is refusing treatment for a life threatening condition, the duty of care would require confidentiality to be breached to the extent of informing those with parental responsibility for the child who might then be able to provide the necessary consent to the treatment.

In other cases, consent should be sought from a person with parental responsibility if such a person is available. It is important to check that persons have proper authority (as parents or guardians). Ideally, there should be notes within the child's file as to any unusual arrangements.[22]

This guidance both reflects the principles contained in the 'refusal cases' and also the positive obligation imposed on the state under Article 2 of the ECHR to protect and preserve life. Reference to a 'life-threatening condition' without further explanation, however, requires clarification. Is this type of condition limited to exceptional circumstances such as a heart transplant case?[23] Alternatively, will the description cover the provision of emergency psychiatric treatment to the young person who does not want to be admitted as an in-patient? It may be more straightforward to signpost that in the rare cases where a competent child is refusing life-saving treatment then issues about breaching the child's rights to confidentiality should be referred immediately to the courts.

---

22   *Confidentiality: NHS Code of Practice*, ante Annex B, paragraphs 9 and 10. This guidance is incorporated in the Department of Health (2007) *Mental Health Act 1983 Draft revised Code of Practice*. London: DH.

23   A 15-year-old girl refused to consent to the heart transplant which was needed to save her life. The girl's reasons for refusing consent were that she did not want to have someone else's heart, and did not wish to take medication for the rest of her life. Her mother consented to the treatment. The judge authorised the hospital to give treatment. *Re M (Medical Treatment)* [1999] 2 FLR 1097.

The child who is not competent/the young person who lacks capacity

If a child is not regarded as Gillick competent then the position is also uncertain.[24] What is the entitlement of children, who are not regarded as Gillick competent, to confidentiality? Where a child lacks capacity to make their own treatment decisions, the person or body with parental responsibility[25] may give consent to medical treatment on the child's behalf. It must follow that to allow treatment to be given effectively, and safely, then this entitlement to consent on behalf of the incapacitated child should also cover authority to disclose confidential medical information about that child. In emergencies confidential information necessary to allow life-saving treatment (or prevent the serious deterioration in the health) of a child can be provided without the consent of the person or body with parental responsibility.

The fact that children's rights to confidentiality may be more limited than the rights of adults does not mean that these rights should not be strenuously protected. The professional's duty of confidentiality to children and young people is the same as their duty to adults.[26]

Conclusions

Information about young people may be used, and disclosed, without their explicit consent to provide their health care. Where the provision of health care is not the determining factor, information may only be disclosed without the competent young person's consent where the law, or a court order, requires it or the public interest justifies disclosure. The public interest justifies disclosure where the child or young person would be at risk of significant harm. In all circumstances the Article 8 entitlement of the child, and his or her parents, must be considered. The interests of the child who may not be competent to consent must also be protected by communication with the person or statutory authority with parental responsibility.

---

24 For a discussion see Montgomery, J. (2003) *Health Care Law*, 2nd edn. Oxford: Oxford University Press, pages 308–311.
25 Parental responsibility is defined in the Children Act 1989, section 3(1).
26 General Medical Council (2007) *0–18 Years: Guidance for all Doctors*. London: GMC, paragraph 21.

Chapter 12

Young People, Consent, Refusal and Psychiatric Treatment

Introduction

Two cases[1] that were decided in the early 1990s had a particular impact on approaches to the management and treatment of children and young people with complex mental health difficulties. (The cases are referred to in this chapter as the 'refusal cases'.) These cases had a disproportionate impact on approaches to the psychiatric treatment of children and young people insofar as they served to confuse, rather than clarify, the law.

The statutes most relevant to this chapter are the Mental Health Act 1983 and the Children Act 1989. Although both statutes have been amended since they were passed, their structure and purpose remains unchanged. The Human Rights Act 1998, which came into force on 2 October 2000, has, however, changed the legal landscape in this area. The Human Rights Act required the courts, and public authorities including mental health professionals, to take into account the European Convention on Human Rights (ECHR) in making decisions about children and young people.

The principles from the refusal cases remain unchallenged, yet over the last 15 years there appears to have been a profound shift in the approach to the statutory and common law frameworks to be used where compulsion is

---

1   *Re R (A Minor) (Wardship: Medical Treatment)* [1991] 4 All ER 177 and *Re W (A Minor)*
     (Medical Treatment) [1992] 4 All ER 627.

being considered in relation to children and young people. The purpose of this chapter is to consider the refusal cases and the changes in law and practice that have taken place following those cases.

The Family Law Reform Act 1969

In 1967 the Latey report[2] identified two particular problems that were increasingly occurring in relation to the medical treatment of young people. The first was when young people were living away from home and wanted urgent medical treatment. Under the law current at the time young people could not be treated unless their parents had been traced and this could cause unnecessary suffering. The second problem arose where the young person would not consent to treatment unless they were given a guarantee that their parents would not be told about the treatment. As a response, the Family Law Reform Act 1969 was passed.

> The consent of a minor who has attained the age of 16 years to any surgical, medical or dental treatment which, in the absence of consent, would constitute a trespass to the person, shall be as effective as it would be if he were of full age; and where a minor has by virtue of this section given an effective consent to any treatment it shall not be necessary to obtain any consent for it from his parent or guardian.[3]

The effect of the Family Law Reform Act was to provide young people over the age of 16 with a statutory right to consent to treatment without the necessity of obtaining parental consent.[4]

The Gillick case (1985)

In 1980 the Department of Health and Social Security issued guidance on family planning services for young people. The guidance implied that in certain cases a doctor could lawfully prescribe contraception for a girl under 16 without her parents' consent. Victoria Gillick, the mother of five daughters under the age of 16, challenged the lawfulness of this advice. Scarman LJ, in concluding that the guidance was lawful, held that:

2   Report of the Committee on the Age of Majority (Cmnd 3342 (1967)).
3   Family Law Reform Act 1969, section 8.
4   Section 8 does not apply to an intervention which is not of direct health benefit to the young person, for example blood donation or non-therapeutic research.

> The parental right to determine whether or not their minor child below the age of 16 will have medical treatment terminates if and when the child achieves sufficient understanding and intelligence to enable him or her to understand fully what is proposed.[5]

He then developed the concept of what has come to be described as 'Gillick competence:'[6]

> There is much that has to be understood by a girl under the age of 16 if she is to have legal capacity to consent to such treatment. It is not enough that she should understand the nature of the advice which is being given: she must also have a sufficient maturity to understand what is involved.[7]

The effect of this case was to allow a child under the age of 16 (16- to 18-year-old young persons being covered by the Family Law Reform Act 1969), providing they were Gillick competent, a right to consent to treatment without the necessity to obtain parental consent.

The cases of R (1991) and W (1992) – the refusal cases

The case of R

R was nearly 16 when the litigation involving her care and treatment commenced. In March 1991, 'anxiety developed about her mental health. She seemed often flat and expressionless and resistant to being touched by anyone. She appeared to experience visual and auditory hallucinations and sometimes suicidal thoughts.'[8]

In May of that year she was regarded as being ill enough to be detained under the Mental Health Act 1983. 'She absconded from the children's home and went back to her own house where she ran amok doing serious damage to the building and furniture. She made a most savage attack on her father and assaulted her mother.' She then experienced substantial swings of

---

5   *Gillick* v. *West Norfolk and Wisbech Area Health Authority and another* [1985] 3 All ER, page 423.

6   In 2006 Victoria Gillick wrote to the author of an article in the BMJ. 'Following correspondence with Victoria Gillick, I am clear that she "has never suggested to anyone, publicly or privately, that [she] disliked being associated with the term "Gillick competent".' Wheeler, R. (2006) 'Gillick or Fraser? A plea for consistency over competence in children.' *British Medical Journal 332*, page 807.

7   *Gillick* v. *West Norfolk and Wisbech Area Health Authority and another* [1985] 3 All ER, page 424.

8   All quotations in this section are from the report of the case of *Re R*, pages 180–181.

mood; the downward swings became serious enough for her to be placed on a section 2 at the beginning of June 1991.

From an adult psychiatric ward at a general hospital she was transferred to a psychiatric unit. She came off section. Then concerns started to grow over her mental health, 'to the extent that serious thought was being given to the use of compulsory medication because she was becoming increasingly defiant'.

On 28 June 1991 the consultant responsible for her care telephoned a social worker (the local authority now had a parental responsibility under a care order). He stated 'that he believed R to be in a psychotic state and that he wanted permission to administer anti-psychotic medication to her'. He told the social worker that R was 'extremely paranoid, becoming extremely argumentative, hostile and accusative'. The local authority consented to medical treatment being given to her. R then spoke to an ASW (for three hours) who concluded that 'he did not regard her as "sectionable"'. The local authority then withdrew their consent to the provision of medication. On 3 July 2001 she was seen by a psychiatrist who concluded:

> she still requires treatment as an in-patient but that she has improved sufficiently for the Mental Health Act not to be relevant… Should she not continue with treatment, her more florid psychotic behaviour is likely to return, and she might become a serious suicidal risk again.

The local authority initiated wardship proceedings.[9] The issue to be decided was whether the court could authorise treatment to which R objected. It was held that the powers of a wardship judge do extend to consent to medical treatment when the child refuses.

Although in this case R was regarded as not being competent (Farquharson LJ referring to the *Gillick* case as being concerned with 'the developing maturity of normal children under the age of 16')[10] the court went on to hold that, even if she had been competent, the court, and her parents, could have overridden her refusal.

---

9 The Children Act 1989, section 100, prevents a child who is in care being a ward of court. The Act was implemented on 14 October 1991 after R had been warded. In the case of *W* the proceedings were commenced after the Children Act had been implemented and, as she was subject to a care order, wardship was not available and, so the inherent jurisdiction was used.

10 *Re R (A Minor) (Wardship: Medical Treatment)* [1991] 4 All ER 177, page 192.

The case of W

W was anorexic. She was subject to a care order. When she was coming up to her 15th birthday she required in-patient treatment in a specialist unit. 'Whilst at the unit [she] displayed violence towards the staff and began injuring herself by picking her skin.'[11]

Her condition deteriorated to the extent that 'for a short time she had to be fed by nasogastric tube and have her arms encased in plaster'.[12] She gradually lost weight and on one occasion she used violence towards a member of staff that required the police to be called. The local authority made an application to the court under the inherent jurisdiction for authority to treat her without her consent.

This case developed, and clarified, the principle first propounded in W.

> No minor of whatever age has power by refusing consent to treatment to override a consent to treatment by someone who has parental responsibility for the minor and a fortiori a consent by the court. Nevertheless such a refusal is a very important consideration in making clinical judgements and for parents and the court in deciding whether themselves to give consent. Its importance increases with the age and maturity of the minor.[13]

The case of K, W and H (1993)

Following the R decision the case of K, W and H[14] came before the court. (Although the case was decided following W, the judgment in the W case was not yet available to the court.) St Andrew's Hospital initiated applications under the Children Act in respect of three children being treated in the hospital. Two of the children were subject to secure accommodation orders; the third child was being treated on the basis of parental responsibility. The hospital had been advised to seek a ruling from the court as to the lawfulness of the treatment on the basis of the complexity of the case. Thorpe J peremptorily dismissed the applications and, following the case of R, he concluded that the law was 'perfectly clear' in this field:

11   Re W (A Minor) (Medical Treatment) [1992] 4 All ER 627, page 630f.
12   Re W (A Minor) (Medical Treatment) [1992] 4 All ER 627, page 630g.
13   Re W (A Minor) (Medical Treatment) [1992] 4 All ER 627, pages 639–640.
14   Re K, W and H (Minors) (Medical Treatment) [1993] 1 FLR 854.

The decision of the Court of Appeal in Re R [above] made it plain that a child with Gillick competence can consent to treatment, but that if he or she declines to do so, consent can be given by someone else who has parental rights or responsibilities.[15]

The effect of the refusal cases

The 'refusal cases' required professionals and their advisers to reconsider the most appropriate intervention where children and young people refused psychiatric treatment. Before these cases the law had appeared reasonably clear, as government guidance published in 1990 demonstrated:

> Where a doctor concludes…that a child under the age of 16 has the capacity to make such a decision for himself (informal admission) there is no right to admit him to hospital informally or to keep him there on an informal basis against his will.

> Young people aged 16–18. Anyone in this age group who is 'capable of expressing his own wishes' can admit or discharge himself as an informal patient to or from hospital, irrespective of the wishes of his parents or guardian.[16]

The 'refusal cases', whilst attempting to clarify the law, in fact had the opposite effect. There now existed a 'complete lack of coherence'[17] between these cases, and the case of *Gillick*. The principle (the 'refusal principle') that the refusal of treatment by a competent child/young person could be over-ridden by a parent, or the court, did not assist the practitioner when it came to the management of the care and treatment of children and young people with complex mental health difficulties.

Not only did the refusal principle fail to protect the rights of the child, it appeared to signpost to professionals that overriding a competent child or young person's opposition to major psychiatric treatment decisions could now take place outside a framework of statutory protection, providing parental consent was obtained.

The principle also took no account of the complex interplay between parent and child where the right of the parent to override their child's refusal

---

15   *Re K, W and H (Minors) (Medical Treatment)* [1993] 1 FLR 854, page 859.
16   Department of Health (1990) *Mental Health Act 1983 Code of Practice*. London: DH, paragraphs 29.5 and 29.6.
17   Fortin, J. (2003) *Children's Rights and the Developing Law*, 2nd edn. London: LexisNexis.

could in fact exacerbate the psychiatric condition that needed to be treated. For example, in some situations the child might, rightly or wrongly, claim that the parents were the cause of their distress.

The Mental Health Act 1983

A more measured approach to these complex cases would have been to have properly evaluated the benefits of using, where appropriate, the Mental Health Act. In R, the court appeared to accept on face value the evidence that the Mental Health Act had no application or relevance to R's predicament. If the use of the Act had been looked at more closely then the following issues might have been considered:

1. R was never properly assessed. Although she spoke to an ASW she was never interviewed in a 'suitable manner'.[18]

2. The statement by the ASW that she was 'not sectionable' was not challenged. Was she not sectionable because she did not meet the criteria for admission set down in the Mental Health Act or was she not sectionable because the professionals did not want to section her?

3. The treating psychiatrist reasoned that R still required treatment as an in-patient, that she was still at significant risk and she was likely not to be compliant with treatment if not subject to compulsion. He then concluded that the use of the Mental Health Act was not justified. The illogicality of his reasoning was not challenged.

In the case of W, Donaldson LJ made the following observations:

> The provisions of the Mental Health Act were not considered in any detail in the course of the argument. Suffice it to say that in some circumstances they authorise treatment despite the objections of the parent, whether minor or adult. Probably they would have had no application to W, but even where they are applicable it may be in the long-term interests of the minor that if the same treatment can be secured upon some other basis, this shall be done. Although mental illness should not be regarded as any different from physical illness, it is not always so viewed by the uninformed and the fact that in later life it

---

18   The phrase 'suitable manner' is contained in the Mental Health Act 1983, section 13(2).

might become known that a minor had been treated under the Acts might rebound to his or her disadvantage.[19]

Donaldson LJ's brief analysis of the Mental Health Act was not accurate. Anorexia nervosa is capable of being a mental disorder within section 1 of the Mental Health Act[20] and therefore the use of the Act could have been considered. The approach to the question of stigma was unduly narrow. Arguably what would stigmatise a young person such as W was not the fact of her detention under the Mental Health Act but rather being labelled as 'mentally ill' and being caught up in the mental health system. W therefore had already been stigmatised by her in-patient treatment for mental disorder.

No clear arguments, therefore, about the availability and utility of the Mental Health Act were presented in either case.[21] If this had happened, then the court would have had to have considered whether the use of the Mental Health Act would have met the best interests of either R or W.

In a case[22] involving the applicability of a secure accommodation order in respect of a 16-year-old young woman suffering from anorexia nervosa, Wall J had to consider whether the existence of a parallel statutory regime required the court to use the statutory route rather than use its inherent powers. He noted that there was no power under the Mental Health Act 'which would enable me to require C to be admitted to hospital as a patient'.[23] He agreed, however, that the court should always consider alternative avenues, particularly at the outset of an application to the court where 'leave' had to be obtained.[24]

In the 'refusal cases', therefore, the benefits conferred by detention under the Mental Health Act, for example statutory safeguards and rights of appeal, were not considered. Even if R and W's detention had been fully considered the law would not have required the use of the Mental Health Act; rather the court in the exercise of its discretion would have been able to

---

19   Re W (A Minor) (Medical Treatment) [1992] 4 All ER 627, page 639.
20   Riverside Mental Health NHS Trust v. Fox [1994] 1 FLR 614.
21   Commentators writing at the time identified the apparent shortcomings in the professionals' approach – for example Fennell, P. (1992) 'Informal compulsion: the psychiatric treatment of juveniles under common law.' Journal of Social Welfare and Family Law 4, pages 311–332.
22   In this case the clinic did not qualify as a hospital with powers of detention under the Mental Health Act and C's treating doctor was 'philosophically opposed to the admission of children to hospital under the Mental Health Act'. Re C (Detention: Medical Treatment) [1997] 2 FLR 180, page 194.
23   Re C (Detention: Medical Treatment) [1997] 2 FLR 180, page 198.
24   Children Act 1989, section 100(3).

properly consider what intervention would have been in the best interests of the children. The use of the Act was, however, barely considered.

Despite the assertion of Thorpe J in *K, W and H*, the law in this area was regarded by most professionals as both confusing and complex[25] and an informed analysis of the use of the Act would have clarified, rather than confused. Why is it that within a decade the use of the Mental Health Act to allow the detention and treatment of children and young people was regarded if not as commonplace, certainly unremarkable?

The Children Act 1989

Assisting professionals in developing clear approaches to complex cases was not helped by confusion surrounding the application of the Children Act. 'Using the Children Act' was (and still is) often imprecisely used to describe a solution to the problems illustrated in the 'refusal cases'. What the phrase appeared to encompass was, first, the right of the child's parents, with their parental responsibility delineated in the Children Act,[26] to make decisions on behalf of their children. Second, the phrase was used to describe a number of overlapping statutory and common law regimes which could include:

1. the use of the wardship or inherent jurisdiction (accessed through procedures contained in the Children Act 1989)

2. applications to the court to make section 8 specific issue orders under the Children Act

3. the use of section 25 secure accommodation orders with, if required, the court making an order in relation to medical treatment under wardship or the inherent jurisdiction.

The Children Act contains a statutory framework which provides for the lawful restriction of a child's liberty.[27] Two statutes therefore exist that allow for the lawful detention of young people with complex mental health difficulties, that is the Mental Health Act and the Children Act. The statutes are

---

25   'The legal framework governing the admission to hospital and treatment of young people under the age of 18 (and in particular those under the age of 16) is complex...' Department of Health (1990) *Mental Health Act 1983 Code of Practice.* London: DH, paragraph 29.3.
26   Children Act 1989, section 3.
27   Ibid., section 25.

not interrelated.[28] The Children Act specifically provides that a child subject to a secure accommodation order cannot at the same time be subject to an order under the Mental Health Act.[29] The purpose of the two statutes is quite different. The Mental Health Act deals primarily with the care and treatment of people with mental disorder. The Children Act 1989:

> brings together in a single coherent legislative framework the private and public law relating to children. It aims to strike a balance between the rights of children to express their views on decisions made about their lives, the rights of parents to exercise their responsibilities towards the child and the duty of the state to intervene where the child's welfare requires it.[30]

In the mid-nineties, however, some of the specialist centres providing secure care and treatment were registered with the relevant registration authorities to allow them both to detain and treat under the Mental Health Act and to restrict the liberty of young people under the Children Act. In the case of *K, W and H* the court referred to the units at St Andrew's as specialising 'in handling cases of highly disturbed adolescents who are generally committed to their care either through Mental Health Act orders or secure accommodation orders'.[31]

Regulations (and these have not been altered) allow a health authority and an NHS trust to make applications under section 25. The same organisations that managed hospitals authorised to take detained patients could also be operating a secure accommodation regime.[32]

Whilst children and young people were being cared for and treated in the same institution under different statutory frameworks it is not surprising, therefore, that the statutory regimes were perceived to be linked. This practice has apparently however largely fallen into misuse with specialist

---

28   There are some specific references in the Mental Health Act to children and young people, for example where the local authority is the nearest relative for a child under a care order. Mental Health Act 1983, section 27.

29   'Section 25 shall not apply to a child who is detained under any provision of the Mental Health Act 1983.' Regulation 5(1), Children Act (Secure Accommodation) Regulations 1991. Connell J held that the purpose of Regulation 5 is to ensure that where criteria under the Mental Health Act 1983 are being considered, and are satisfied, it is not necessary to consider whether an order under section 25 should be made. *Hereford and Worcester County Council* v. *S* [1993] 2 FLR 360.

30   *The Children Act 1989 Guidance and Regulations* (1991), Volume 1. London: HMSO 1991, paragraph 1.1.

31   *Re K, W and H (Minors) (Medical Treatment)* [1993] 1 FLR 854, page 855.

32   Children (Secure Accommodation) (No 2) Regulations 1991.

treatment centres now requiring the use of the Mental Health Act when the use of a statutory framework is considered to be justified.

In reality there are differences between the characteristics of the population of secure units compared to specialist psychiatric centres. Also the purpose of 'detention' under the MHA is different to that of 'detention' under section 25:

> When considering which provisions to use [Mental Health Act or Children Act] it is particularly important to identify the primary purpose of the proposed intervention. For example, a serious mentally ill child may require treatment under the Act, whereas the needs of a behaviourally disturbed child may be more appropriately met within secure accommodation under the Children Act.[33]

These differences are now firmly embedded in the culture of health and social services authorities, respectively. This has largely eroded any notion of 'choice' between the two statutory regimes.

Demographics and economics

The uncertainty generated by the 'refusal cases' together with a lack of clarity concerning the application of the statutory regimes applicable to the care and treatment of children and young people with mental health difficulties contributed to delay in developing clear ways of managing complex cases.

The need to address the problem is likely to have been spurred on by demographic change. Although there is no clear data concerning trends over the last decade, there is some indication that the number of children and young people admitted both to specialist psychiatric units and to adult units has increased.[34] The reasons for this increase are unclear. The following factors, however, may be significant: the increasing prevalence and recognition of mental disorder identified in children and young people and the increase in the number of residential facilities (particularly in the private

---

33   Department of Health (1999) *Mental Health Act 1983 Code of Practice.* London: DH, paragraph 31.3.

34   In 1996 Brenda Hoggett (now Lady Justice Hale) wrote: 'Mental Health Act compulsion is hardly ever used for patients under the age of 16.' Hoggett, B. (1996) *Mental Health Law.* London: Sweet & Maxwell, page 63. The section on the MHAC (Chapter 4) refers to data collated by the Commission with the most recent information from a March 2007 census. The census does not provide a breakdown of the ages of the 898 under-18s who were resident in hospitals, or the one third of that group who were detained.

sector) to care for and treat them. Statutory frameworks, section 25 of the Children Act and Mental Health Act detention provided alternatives to expensive applications to the High Court and provided process rights and independent review.

Particular concerns have been expressed over a number of years by organisations such as the Mental Health Act Commission, The Royal College of Psychiatrists, the Children's Commissioner and Young Minds about the practice of admitting children and young people to adult psychiatric facilities. The government's response to these concerns has been various including the introduction of a notification procedure[35] where a child under 16 is placed on an adult psychiatric ward and amending the Mental Health Act to reduce the unacceptable use of adult wards for a child/young person under the age of 18.[36]

The Human Rights Act 1998

The Act became operational in 2000 and since then mental health professionals have become increasingly aware of the requirements placed upon them not to act in ways which are incompatible with the Convention rights of the children and young people with whom they work.[37]

Where a child or young person refuses psychiatric treatment and as a consequence measures of compulsion are required the Convention rights that are most likely to be engaged are Articles 5 and 8. Article 5, the right to liberty and security, will apply when a child or young person is deprived of their liberty. Article 8, the right to respect for private and family life, will apply when a parent consents to treatment on behalf of a child.

The distinction between deprivation of liberty and restriction of movement was not regarded as being particularly relevant in the refusal cases; these cases were decided prior to the Human Rights Act coming into force. The effect of the Act being in force is that in future the courts (and

---

35   'In the exceptional case where a child of 16 or under is placed on an adult psychiatric ward, SHAs should use the Serious Untoward Incident protocol to notify the Department of Health setting out how the child will be moved to appropriate accommodation within 48 hours and how the ward and staffing have been made appropriate for the child's needs.' Letter dated 29 June 2007 Department of Health to Strategic Health Authority Chief Executives Gateway Number: 8390.

36   Section 131A Mental Health Act 1983 – see chapter 4 page 63.

37   Human Rights Act 1998, section 6(1).

public authorities) must take into account ECHR principles, and in particular the distinction between deprivation of liberty and restriction of movement.

The particular relevance of this is that from 2000 onwards mental health professionals and their advisers had to place ECHR considerations at the heart of their decision making. The common law principle enunciated in the 'refusal cases' was no longer adequate to protect the interests of the children and young people at the centre of disputes about compulsory treatment, particularly where deprivation of liberty was a central issue.

Changing the law

Since the refusal cases were decided, attitudes toward parental authority and children's rights have changed. This change was specifically reflected in the consideration that governments and their advisers were giving to changing mental health legislation.

By 2000 the government had identified that there needed to be special provision in mental health legislation for children and young people. In the Green Paper that presaged the (now defunct) draft Mental Health Bill, the government proposed that a 16- to 18-year-old refusing treatment should only be treated under compulsory powers, removing the right of parents to override the refusal. Referring to the development over recent years of an increasing recognition of the capacity of a developing young person to take decisions on his or her own behalf the Green Paper stated:

> In the case of a young person, care and treatment for mental disorder, without his or her consent, can raise complex ethical problems for the clinical teams and be stressful for all concerned. There is a particular problem if that care, sometimes over a sustained period of time, requires restraint or seclusion or the administration of medication against the young person's wishes. In these circumstances it may well be in the best interests of the young person for care and treatment to be provided within the framework of mental health legislation. But the correct interpretation of the law in these circumstances is often difficult. There is no requirement, if the young person's parents agree to treatment, to treat him or her under compulsory powers in the 1983 Act.[38]

---

38 Secretary of State for Health and the Home Secretary (2000) *Reforming the Mental Health Act. Part 1: The New Legal Framework.* Cm 5016–1. London: TSO, paragraph 3.71.

The Mental Health Act 2007 amends section 131 of the Mental Health Act 1983. (See Chapter 4.) The effect of this amendment is that a 16- or 17-year-old who has capacity may decide whether or not to be admitted to hospital for treatment for mental disorder regardless of the fact that there is a person with parental responsibility for him or her. If the young person refuses then this refusal cannot be overridden.

Although the position of capable 16- and 17-year-olds in relation to the refusal of treatment has been clarified, the position of incapacitated 16- and 17-year-olds and the under 16s remains less clear. In relation to incapacitated 16- and 17-year-olds the provisions of the Mental Capacity Act 2005 will apply. This means that treatment falling short of deprivation of liberty would be lawful providing the treatment is in the young person's best interests.[39]

Changing advice

The Draft Code of Practice,[40] currently the subject of consultation, provides the following advice in relation to children who are less than 16 years old and who lack competence to consent:

> If the decision is not within the parental zone of responsibility or the consent of a person with parental responsibility is not given the Mental Health Act should be used as long as the child meets the conditions for admission set out in the Act.[41]

The Draft Code does not contain such coherent advice in relation to the situation where the Gillick-competent child refuses medical treatment:

> It would be prudent, to obtain a court declaration or decision if faced with a competent child or young person who is refusing to consent to treatment, to determine whether it is lawful to treat the patient on the basis of the consent of a person with parental responsibility or whether the Mental Health Act should be used instead.[42]

---

39   Department for Constitutional Affairs (2007) *Mental Capacity Act 2005 Code of Practice.* London: TSO, Chapter 12.
40   Department of Health (2007) *Mental Health Act 1983 Draft revised Code of Practice.* London: DH.
41   Ibid., paragraph 39.24.
42   Ibid., paragraph 39.36.

When the completed Code is published it is to be hoped that the government return to the advice contained in the draft illustrative Code (the precursor to the Draft Code) which dealt with the problem clearly and succinctly:

> To put it simply, their [competent children under 18] decisions to consent to treatment or to refuse treatment should not be over-ridden by a person with parental responsibility.[43]

Conclusions

The 'refusal' doctrine enunciated by the courts in the early 1990s had the effect of making the law surrounding the care and treatment of young people with complex mental health difficulties unnecessarily confusing and difficult. Misunderstandings about the application of the Children Act did not assist. The scope and purpose of the Mental Health Act was not always understood, in particular that it applied to persons of any age and provided a protective framework for state intervention.

A growing number of children and young people needing treatment in psychiatric hospitals required that the law in this area be reviewed and clarified.

The Human Rights Act required there to be a focus on the need for statutory protection in particular where deprivation of liberty was being considered or used. (The focus on Article 5 may obscure other areas of psychiatric treatment which fall short of 'deprivation of liberty', for example nasogastric tube feeding of anorexic children.) There has also been increasing recognition over recent years of the rights of young people to make their own decisions.

The law in this area is now gradually catching up with changing social attitudes. The Mental Health Act 1983 is now amended so that 16- to 18-year-olds who refuse medical treatment for mental disorder can only be treated under compulsory powers and will therefore benefit from statutory protection.

The position of the under 16s remains much less certain; however, an increasing awareness of the need to protect this age group should impact on all aspects of decision making concerning their care and treatment.

---

43   Department of Health (2007) Mental Health Act 1983 (Draft Illustrative Code. London DH Paragraph 31.42).

Appendix 1
Further Reading

Children's rights

Fortin, J. (2003) *Children's Rights and the Developing Law*, 2nd edition. London: Butterworths. This book contains a detailed analysis of the law in the domestic and international context.

Health care and medical treatment

Montgomery J. (2003) *Health Care Law*, 2nd edition. Oxford: Oxford University Press. A good introductory text.

Butler-Sloss, L.J.E. and Harper, R.S. (1999) *Medical Treatment and the Law: The Protection of Adults and Minors in the Family Division*. Bristol: Jordan Publishing. Although dated, this book covers the law both in relation to adults and children.

BMA (2001) Consent, Rights and Choices in Health Care for Children and Young People. London: BMJ Books. A readable and non-technical book that identifies and discusses law and ethics.

Children's law

White, N., Lowe, R. and Lowe, A.P. (2002) *The Children Act in Practice*, 3rd edition. London: Butterworths. This is now out-of-date; however a fourth edition is due in September 2008.

McFarlane, A. and Reardon, M. (2006) *Child Care and Adoption Law: A Practical Guide*. Bristol: Jordan Publishing. An up-to-date book on adoption law.

Mental health law

Jones, R. (2006) *Mental Health Act Manual*, 10th edition. London: Sweet & Maxwell. Where mental health professionals need a book to provide them with an authoritative guide to every aspect of the Mental Health Act 1983 they turn this book. Although not always an easy book to use (the reader may find it confusing without some prior knowledge of the structure of the Act), it remains the best available up-to-date text in this area and contains a wealth of detailed and informed commentary.

Bartlett, P. and Sandland, R. (2007) *Mental Health Law: Policy and Practice*, 3rd edition. Oxford: Oxford University Press. This is the most readable academic text on this subject and contextualises both mental health and capacity law.

Hoggett, B. (1996) *Mental Health Law*, 4th edition. London: Sweet & Maxwell. Although dated, this book still repays detailed reference because of its scope and originality.

Eldergill, E. (1997) *Mental Health Review Tribunals: Law and Practice*. London: Sweet & Maxwell. Although dated, this book still repays detailed reference because of its scope and originality.

Brown, R. (2006) *The Approved Social Worker's Guide to Mental Health Law*. Exeter: Learning Matters. A more general guide for ASWs.

Hewitt, D. (2007) *The Nearest Relative Handbook*. London: Jessica Kingsley Publishers. This book contains all that one could possibly want to know about the nearest relative.

Two books on the Mental Health Act 2007 have already been published:

Bowen, P. (2008) *Blackstone's Guide to the Mental Health Act*. Oxford: Oxford University Press.

Fennell, P. (2007) *Mental Health (Jordan's New Law)*. Bristol: Jordan Publishing.

Criminal justice

Ashford, M., Chard, A. and Redhouse, N. (2006) *Defending Young People in the Criminal Justice System*. London: Legal Action Group. This is the only book that needs to be referred to if the practitioner wants to know more about this area of law. It contains a chapter entitled 'Parental Involvement' which details the responsibilities placed on parents who have children within the criminal justice system.

Mental Capacity Act

Jones, R. (2007) *Mental Capacity Act Manual*, 2nd edition. London: Sweet & Maxwell. An annotated version of the Act with commentary.

Bartlett, P. (2008) *Blackstone's Guide to the Mental Capacity Act 2005*, 2nd edition. Oxford: Oxford University Press. A more academic and discursive approach to the Act.

Brown, R. and Barber, P. (2008) *The Social Worker's Guide to Mental Capacity Law*. Exeter: Learning Matters. A book on the Act aimed primarily at qualified social workers.

Service provision

Read, J., Clements, L. and Ruebain, D. (2006) *Disabled Children and the Law: Research and Good Practice*, 2nd edition. London: Jessica Kingsley Publishers. The most comprehensive book in this area in relation children and young people.

Clements, L. and Thompson, P. (2007) *Community Care and the Law*, 4th edition. London: Legal Action Group. This contains a useful chapter on the Children Act and duties to children in need.

Diagnosis and management of complex mental illness

Kaplan, P.S. (1998) *A Child's Odyssey: Child and Adolescent Development.* West Publishing. An excellent overview of child and adolescent development.

Garrala, M.E. and Hyde, C. (2003) *Managing Children with Psychiatric Problems*, 2nd edition. Oxford: Wiley Blackwell. A useful and concise summary of psychiatric disorder in children and adolescents and the services available to support them.

Thompson, M., Cooper, M. and Hooper, C.M. (2005) *Child and Adolescent Mental Health: Theory and Practice.* London: Hodder Arnold. A comprehensive and readable text put together by multiple authors to represent child and adolescent psychiatric disorder and the health services that currently exist.

Harrington, R. (1993) *Depressive Disorder in Childhood and Adolescence (Wiley Series on Studies in Child Psychiatry).* Chichester: John Wiley & Sons. A classic text.

BMA (2006) 'Child and Adolescent Mental Health: A Guide for Health Care Professionals.' Available at www.bma.org.uk/ap.nsf/content/Childadolescentmentalhealth. This gives a very helpful overview.

Extract from Local Authority Circular (99)29

Care Plans and Care Proceedings under the Children Act 1989

Structure and contents of the care plan

12. The advised contents of the care plan items are set out within a structure of five sections:

Overall aim

Child's needs including contact

Views of others

Placement details and timetable

Management and support by local authority

13. The complete list of matters that the guidance advises should be included within each of the care plan's five sections is as follows:

Section 1: Overall aim

1.1   Aim of the plan and summary of timetable

Section 2: Child's needs including contact

2.1   The child's identified needs, including needs arising from race, culture, religion or language, special education, health or disability

2.2   The extent to which the wishes and views of the child have been obtained and acted upon; and

2.3 The reasons for supporting this or explanations of why wishes/views have not been given absolute precedence

2.4 Summary of how those needs might be met

2.5 Arrangements for, and purpose of, contact in meeting the child's needs (specifying contact relationship, e.g. parent, step-parent, other family member, former carer, friend, siblings, including those looked after who may have a separate placement); any proposals to restrict or terminate contact.

Section 3: Views of others

3.1 The extent to which the wishes and views of the child's parents and anyone else with a sufficient interest in the child (including representatives of other agencies, current and former carers) have been obtained and acted upon, and

3.2 The reasons for supporting them or explanations of why wishes/views have been given absolute precedence.

Section 4: Placement details and timetable

4.1 Proposed placement – type and details (or details of alternative placements)

4.2 Time that is likely to elapse before proposed placement is made

4.3 Likely duration of placement (or other placement)

4.4 Arrangements for health care (including consent to examination and treatment)

4.5 Arrangements for education (including any pre-school day care/activity)

4.6 Arrangements for reunification (often known as 'rehabilitation') (see also 4.8)

4.7 Other services to be provided to the child

4.8 Other services to be provided to parents and other family members

4.9 Details of proposed support services in placement for the carers

4.10 Specific details of the parents' role in day-to-day arrangements.

Section 5: Management and support by local authority

5.1 Who is to be responsible for implementing the overall plan

5.2 Who is to be responsible for implementing specific tasks within the plan

5.3 Dates of review

5.4 Contingency plan, if placement breaks down or if preferred placement is not available

5.5 Arrangements for input by parents, the child and others into the ongoing decision-making process

5.6 Arrangements for notifying the responsible authority of disagreements about the implementation of the care plan or making representations or complaints.

Appendix 3

The 2007 Mental Health Act Draft revised Code of Practice: Chapter 39 – Children and Young People under the Age of 18

Chapter 39 – Children and Young People under the Age of 18

39.1 This chapter provides guidance to mental health professionals working with children (less than 16 years old) and young people (16 or 17 years old) with complex mental disorders. A number of statutes make provision relating to the treatment of children and young people suffering from mental disorder and this may lead to some uncertainty. This chapter clarifies the legal frameworks and gives practical guidance on dealing with common difficulties.

The legal framework and guidance

39.2 There is no minimum age limit for admission to hospital and for a community treatment order under the Mental Health Act (but only a person who is at least 16 years old can be subject to guardianship).

39.3 The legal framework governing the admission to hospital and treatment of children is complex. It is the responsibility of all relevant professionals, local social services authorities, education authorities and NHS bodies to ensure that necessary information is available to all those responsible for the care of children and young people and they are familiar with the relevant legislation and guidance.

Special needs of children and young people

39.4 Specialist child and adolescent mental health services (CAMHS) are designed to provide treatment to children and young people suffering from mental disorder. It is important that CAMHS are fully involved with the care of children and young people from their initial assessment and that the special needs of children and young people are recognised as follows.

Mental health assessment

39.5 At least one of the people involved in the assessment of a person who is less than 18 years old, i.e. one of the two medical practitioners or the AMHP, should be a clinician specialising in CAMHS. Where this is not possible, a CAMHS clinician should be consulted as soon as possible. See Chapter 4 for fuller information on the assessment process.

Responsible clinician and others caring and treating under 18s

39.6 Where possible those responsible for the care and treatment of children and young people should be child specialists. Where this is not possible, it is good practice for the clinical staff to have access to a CAMHS specialist for advice and consultation.

Age-appropriate facilities

39.7 Children and young people admitted to hospital for the treatment of mental disorder should be accommodated in an environment that is suitable for their age (subject to their needs).

Education

39.8 All children, including patients who are 16 or 17 years old who wish to continue their education, should not be denied access to learning merely because they are receiving medical treatment for a mental health condition (see 39.46 for further information).

Guiding principles

39.9 The guiding principles set out in Chapter 1 applies equally to children and young people although in their cases there will be special considerations. In particular:

- The best interests of the child and young person must always be considered.

- Children and young people should always be kept as fully informed as possible, just as an adult would, and should receive clear and detailed information concerning their care and treatment.

- The child and young person's views, wishes and feelings should always be considered as seriously as those of an adult.

- Any intervention in the life of a child or young person considered necessary by reason of their mental disorder should be the least restrictive and least stigmatising option consistent with effective care and treatment but also should result in the least possible separation from family, carers, friends and community or interruption of their education as is consistent with their well-being.

- All children and young people should receive equal access to education provision as their peers.

- Children and young people have as much right to expect their dignity to be respected as anyone else.

- The privacy and confidentiality of all children and young people should be respected unless sharing information about them is necessary.

- Determining the most appropriate form of care.

39.10 Where the primary purpose of the intervention is not to provide medical treatment for mental disorder, but the intervention requires the detention of the child or young person, consideration should be given to using section 25 of the Children Act 1989 (see the flow charts after paragraph 39.58).

39.11 For example, if a child or young person was seriously mentally ill they may require treatment under the Mental Health Act, whereas if they were behaviourally disturbed their needs might be more appropriately met within secure accommodation under the Children Act. Professional staff who address these questions should:

- be aware of the relevant statutory provisions and have easy access to competent legal advice

- keep in mind the importance of ensuring that the care and treatment of the child or young person is managed with clarity, consistency and within a recognisable framework; and

- attempt to select the option that reflects the predominant needs of the child or young person at that time whether that be to provide specific mental health care and treatment or to achieve a measure of safety and protection. Either way the least restrictive option consistent with the care and treatment objectives for the child or young person should be sought.

Determining the authority to treat a child or young person for mental disorder informally in hospital

39.12 Determining the authority for treating a child who needs treatment for mental disorder in hospital can be complicated in view of the different scenarios that can arise. In order to assist practitioners flow charts are appended to use in conjunction with the main text and examples are also provided.

Children who are less than 16 years old – the concept of Gillick competence

39.13 In the case of *Gillick*, the court held that children who have sufficient understanding and intelligence to enable them to understand fully what is involved in a proposed intervention will also have the competence to consent to that intervention. This is sometimes described as being 'Gillick competent'. A child may be Gillick competent to consent to medical treatment, research, or any other activity that requires their consent.

39.14 The concept of Gillick competence is said to reflect the child's increasing development to maturity. The understanding required for different interventions will vary considerably. As such a child may have the competence to consent to some interventions but not others. The child's competence to consent should be assessed carefully in relation to each decision that needs to be made.

39.15 In some cases, for example because of a mental disorder, a child's mental state may fluctuate significantly so that on some occasions the child appears Gillick competent in respect of a particular decision and on other occasions does not. In cases such as these, careful consideration should be given to whether the child is truly Gillick competent at any time to take a relevant decision.

39.16 If the child is Gillick competent and is able to give voluntary consent after receiving appropriate information, that consent will be valid and additional consent by a person with parental responsibility will not be required. It is, however, good practice to involve the child's family in the decision-making process, if the child consents to their information being shared.

39.17 Where a child who is Gillick competent (and has the ability to make a decision on their health care) consents to treatment they should be admitted as an informal patient and treated accordingly.

39.18 Paragraph(s) 39.28 below deal with the situation where a Gillick competent child refuses medical treatment.

Children who are less than 16 years old and who lack competence to consent

39.19 Where a child is not Gillick competent then it will usually be possible for a person with parental responsibility to consent to treatment on their behalf If the primary purpose of the intervention is to provide medical treatment for mental disorder in hospital on an informal basis. If however recourse may be needed to compulsory powers, but the primary purpose of the intervention is to protect the child from harm rather than to provide medical treatment, then consideration should be given to using section 25 of the Children Act rather than relying on the Mental Health Act. See paragraph 39.42 below for more information on parental responsibility.

39.20 Before relying on parental consent in relation to a child who is less than 16 years old and who is not Gillick competent, an assessment should be made of whether the matter is within the zone of parental responsibility (see paras. 39.42 and 39.37 below).

39.21 A child's views should be taken into account, even if they are not Gillick competent. How much weight the child's views should be given will depend on how mature the child is. Where a child has been Gillick competent to make a decision but then loses competence any views he expressed before losing competence should be taken into account and may act as parameters limiting the zone of parental responsibility (see paragraph 39.42). For example, if a child has an expressed willingness to receive one form of treatment but not another whilst Gillick competent and he then loses competence it might not be appropriate to give the treatment previously refused to the child as an informal patient even if a person with parental responsibility consents.

39.22 If the decision regarding the treatment of a child (including how the child is to be kept safely in one place) is within the zone of parental responsibility and consent is given by a person with parental responsibility, then the clinician may rely on that consent and treat on that basis as an informal patient.

39.23 The fact that parents or other person has informally admitted a child with parental responsibility should not lead professionals to assume that they have consented to all components of a treatment programme regarded as 'necessary'. Consent should be sought for each aspect of the child's care and treatment as it arises. 'Blanket' consent forms should not be used.

39.24 If the decision is not within the parental zone of responsibility or the consent of a person with parental responsibility is not given, the Mental Health Act should be used so long as the child meets the conditions for admission set out in the Act. Alternatively, it would be possible to treat a child informally on the basis of an order made by the court under its inherent jurisdiction, or by way of an order made under section 8 of the Children Act but it is not likely that there will be much recourse to the courts for authorisation where there is the statutory alternative of treating under the Mental Health Act.

Patients who are 16 or 17 years old and have capacity to consent

39.25 By virtue of section 8 of the Family Law Reform Act 1969, people who are 16 or 17 years old are presumed to be capable of consenting to their own medical treatment, and any ancillary procedures involved in that treatment, such as an anaesthetic. As for adults, consent will be valid only if it is given voluntarily by an appropriately informed patient capable of consenting to the particular intervention. However, unlike adults, the refusal of a competent person aged 16–17 may in certain circumstances be over-ridden by either a person with parental responsibility or a court (see below).

39.26 Section 8 of the Family Law Reform Act applies only to the young person's own treatment. It does not apply to an intervention which is not potentially of direct health benefit to the young person, such as non-therapeutic research on the causes of a disorder. However, a young person may be able to consent to such an intervention under the standard of Gillick competence.

39.27 Section 131 of the Mental Health Act itself provides that where a patient who is 16 or 17 years old has capacity to consent to being admitted for treatment for mental disorder to hospital, they may consent or not consent to being admitted, regardless of the views of a person with parental responsibility. This means that where a young person who is 16 or 17 years old (who has the capacity to make a decision on their health care) consents to being admitted for treatment they should be treated as an informal patient in accordance with section 131, even if a person with parental responsibility is refusing consent.

39.28 In order to establish whether a young person aged 16 or 17 has the requisite capacity to consent to the proposed intervention, the same criteria as for adults should be used. An assessment of a person's capacity must be based on their ability to make a specific decision at the time it needs to be made, and not their ability to make decisions in general. A person is unable to make a decision if they cannot do one or more of the following things:

- understand the information given to them that is relevant to the decision

- retain that information long enough to be able to make the decision

- use or weigh up the information as part of the decision-making process; and

- communicate their decision – this could be by talking or using sign language and includes simple muscle movements such as blinking an eye or squeezing a hand.

39.29 The Mental Capacity Act includes the following and other principles – that 'A person must be assumed to have capacity unless it is established that he lacks capacity,' and that 'A person is not to be treated as unable to make a decision unless all practicable steps to help him to do so have been taken without success.' The Act also states that a lack of capacity cannot be established merely by reference to a person's age or appearance or a condition of his, or an aspect of his behaviour, which might lead others to make unjustified assumptions about his capacity.

39.30 It may be unclear whether a young person lacks capacity within the meaning of the Mental Capacity Act. In those circumstances, it would be prudent to seek a declaration from the court. More information on how the Act applies to young people is given in the Mental Capacity Act Code of Practice.

39.31 If the young person is capable of giving valid consent, then it is not legally necessary to obtain consent from a person with parental responsibility for the young person in addition to that of the young person themselves. It is, however, good practice to involve the young person's family in the decision-making process, unless the young person specifically wishes to exclude them if the young person consents to their information being shared.

39.32 Paragraphs 39.34 onwards deal with the situation where a young person with capacity refuses medical treatment or refuses admission for treatment for mental disorder.

Patients who are 16 or 17 years old and who lack capacity to consent

39.33 If a young person lacks capacity because of an impairment of, or a disturbance in the functioning of, the mind or brain then the Mental Capacity Act will apply in the same way as it does to those who are 18 and over (see Mental Capacity Act code of practice), unless the treatment amounts to a deprivation of liberty in which case see below. If, however, the young person is unable to make the decision for some other reason, for example because they are overwhelmed by the implications of the decision, the Act will not apply to them and the legality of any treatment should be assessed under common law principles. In either case, a person with parental responsibility for the young person could consent to the treatment if the matter is within the parental zone of responsibility. It would however be prudent to seek a declaration from the court before relying on parental consent.

Child or young person with capacity refusing treatment

39.34 Section 131 means that where a young person of 16 or 17 with capacity is refusing to be admitted for treatment for mental disorder in hospital, they cannot be treated informally on the basis of the consent of a person with parental responsibility. Where such a young person, or a Gillick competent child, refuses treatment, it is possible that such a refusal could be over-ruled if it would in all probability lead to the death of that person or to severe permanent injury.

39.35 The courts have, in the past, also found that parents can consent to their competent child being treated even where the child is refusing treatment. This does not apply to the decision of a young person to be admitted to hospital for treatment for mental disorder.

39.36 For other cases, so long as there is no post-Human Rights Act 1998 authority for this proposition, it would be prudent, to obtain a court declaration or decision if faced with a competent child or young person who is refusing to consent to treatment, to determine whether it is lawful to treat the patient on the basis of the consent of a person with parental responsibility or whether the Mental Health Act should be used instead.

Emergency treatment

39.37 A life-threatening emergency may arise when the patient is competent but refuses to consent and consultation with either a person with parental responsibility or the court is impossible, or the persons with parental responsibility refuse consent despite such emergency treatment appearing to be in the best interests of the young person. In such cases, the courts have stated that doubt should be resolved in favour of the preservation of life and it will be acceptable to undertake treatment to preserve life or prevent serious damage to health.

People with parental responsibility

39.38 Those with parental responsibility will often, but not always, be the parents of the child or young person. Legally, the mental health professional only need consent from one person with parental responsibility to treat a child or young person, although clearly it is good practice to involve all those close to the child or young person in the decision-making process. However, if one person with parental responsibility strongly disagreed and was likely to challenge the decision in court, the hospital might wish to consider going to court itself.

39.39 It is essential that those responsible for the care and treatment of the child or young person are clear about who has parental responsibility and always request copies of any court orders for reference on the child or young person's medical or social service file. These orders may include care orders, residence orders, contact orders, evidence of appointment as the child or young person's guardian, parental responsibility agreements or orders under section 4 of the Children Act and any order under wardship.

39.40 If the child or young person is living with either of the parents who are separated, whether there is a residence order and if so in whose favour. It may be necessary to consider whether it is appropriate to contact both parents.

Children looked after by the local authority

39.41 Where children or young people are looked after by the local authority (see section 22 of the Children Act 1989), treatment decisions should usually be discussed with the parent or other person with parental responsibility who continue to have parental responsibility for the child. This might not be the case where there were allegations of abuse by a person with parental responsibility. If a child or young person is voluntarily accommodated by the local authority, the consent of the parent or other person with parental responsibility to the proposed treatment will be required if the child or young person is to be treated informally unless the child is Gillick competent, or the young person has the capacity to make the decision, and that child or young person decides for himself. If the child or young person is subject to a care order, the parents share parental responsibility with the local authority and it will be a matter for negotiation and agreement between them as to who should be consulted although it should be remembered that local authorities can, in the exercise of their powers under section 33(3)(b) of the Children Act, limit the extent to which parents may exercise their parental responsibility.

Parental zone of responsibility

39.42 The 'parental zone of responsibility' is a term covering the matters in relation to which parents may make decisions about the care and treatment of their children and, more specifically, in relation to which the consent of those parents may be relied upon by mental health professionals as giving the necessary authorisation for a particular intervention.

39.43 In assessing whether a particular decision falls within this parental zone of responsibility, two key questions must be answered:

- Firstly, is the decision one which a parent would be expected to make, having regard both to what is considered to be normal practice in our society and to any relevant human rights decisions made by the courts?

- Secondly, are there indications that the parent might not act in the best interests of the child? The less confident a practitioner is that they can answer both questions in the affirmative, the more likely it will be that the decision in question falls outside the zone.

39.44 Clearly, the parameters of the zone will vary from one case to the next: they are determined not only by social norms, but also by the circumstances and dynamics of a specific parent and child. In assessing where the boundaries lie in any particular case, and so whether a parent's consent may be relied upon, mental health professionals might find it helpful to consider the following factors:

- the nature and invasiveness of what is to be done to the child (including the extent to which the child's liberty will be curtailed) – the more extreme the intervention, the more likely it will be that it falls outside the zone

- whether the child is resisting – treating a child that is resisting needs more justification

- general social standards in force at the time as to the sorts of decisions it is acceptable for parents to make – anything that goes beyond the kind of decisions parents routinely make will be more suspect

- the age and maturity of the child – the greater this is, the more likely it will be that it should be the child who is taking the decision and

- the extent to which a parent's interest may conflict with those of the child – this may suggest the parent will not act in the best interests of the child.

39.45 For example, it may be within the zone of parental responsibility for a parent to consent to treatment of a 15 year old child against their will for an eating disorder (where the nature of their disorder means they are unable to consent or refuse the treatment for themselves). However, if force feeding was required by means of invasive treatment in the form of a gastric tube, it might be considered that the extremity of the treatment took it outside the kind of treatment to which a parent could give consent. The child might need to be detained under the Mental Health Act rather than treated as an informal patient.

Age-appropriate services

39.46 Children and young people admitted to hospital for the treatment of mental disorder should be accommodated in an environment that is suitable for their age (subject to their needs). This means that children and young people should have appropriate physical facilities; staff with the right training to understand and address their specific needs as children and young people; and a hospital routine that will allow their personal, social and educational development to continue as normally as possible. This should ensure that children and young persons have equal access to educational opportunities as their peers, in so far as that is consistent with their ability to make use of them, considering their mental state.

39.47 Hospital managers must ensure that the environment is suitable and in reaching their determination must consult a person they consider to be suitable as experienced in child and adolescent mental health services cases.

39.48 If, exceptionally, this is not possible, discrete accommodation in an adult ward, with facilities, security and staffing appropriate to the needs of the child, might provide the most satisfactory solution. Where possible all those involved in the care and treatment of children and young persons should be child specialists. They must always be criminal record background (CRB) vetted. Where it is not possible to have a CAMHS specialist in charge of the child or young person's treatment, arrangements should be made for the clinical staff caring for the child or young person to have access to a CAMHS specialist professional for advice and consultation.

39.49 In a small number of cases the patient's need to be accommodated in a safe environment could, in the short term, take precedence over the suitability of that environment for their age. Furthermore, it is also important to recognise that there is a clear difference between what is a suitable environment for a child or young person in an emergency situation and what is a suitable environment for a child or young person on a longer term basis. In an emergency, such as when the patient is in crisis, the important thing is that the patient is in a safe environment. Once the initial emergency situation has subsided, in determining whether the environment continued to be suitable, the hospital managers would need to consider issues such as whether the patient can mix with individuals of their own age, receive visitors of all ages, and have access to education. Hospital managers have a duty to consider whether a patient should be transferred to more appropriate accommodation and, if so, for this to be arranged as soon as possible.

39.50 Where a young patient's presence on a ward with other children and young people might have a detrimental effect on the other young patients, the hospital managers need to ensure that the interests of other patients are protected. However, the needs of other patients should not override the need to provide accommodation in an environment that is suitable for their age (subject to their needs) for an individual patient aged under 18.

Education

39.51 All children, and 16 or 17 year old patients who wish to continue their education, should not be denied access to learning merely because they are receiving medical treatment for a mental health condition. The duties on local authorities are set out in the Education Act 1996 which also includes powers for local authorities to make provision for young people 16 to 19 years old who are unable to attend school for medical reasons.

Mental Health Review Tribunal

39.52 When children and young people are detained under the Mental Health Act they have the same rights as other patients to apply to the MHRT. Hospital managers should actively promote that an application is made to the MHRT by the child or young person, particularly following their initial detention. It is important that children and young persons are given assistance so that they get access to legal representation at an early stage. In addition hospital managers should bear in mind that their duties to refer patients to the MHRT are different in respect of patients who are less than 18 years old. Where older patients must be referred after a three year period without a tribunal hearing, children and young people must be referred after one year.

Supervised community treatment

39.53 There is no lower age limit for supervised community treatment. The number of children and young people whose clinical and family circumstances make them suitable for supervised community treatment is likely to be small but it should be used where appropriate. See chapter 28 for fuller information on supervised community treatment.

ECT

39.54 ECT is only appropriate for a very small number of children and young people. See paragraph 25.35 and chapter 25 for further information on the process to be undertaken when ECT is being considered for a patient.

Confidentiality

39.55 All children and young people have a right to confidentiality. Gillick competent under 16s and young people aged 16 or 17 are entitled to make decisions about the use and disclosure of information they have provided in confidence in the same way as adults, e.g. they may be receiving treatment or counselling about which they do not want their parents to know. However, where a competent young person or child is refusing treatment for a life threatening condition, the duty of care would require confidentiality to be breached to the extent of informing those with parental responsibility who might then be able to provide the necessary consent to the treatment.

Duties of local authorities in relation to hospital patients

39.56 Local authorities should ensure that they arrange for visits to be made to:

- children and young people looked after by them whether or not under a care order who are in hospital; and

- those accommodated or intended to be accommodated for three months or more by NHS bodies, local education authorities or in residential care, nursing or mental nursing homes (see Review of Children's Cases Regulations 1991 S. I. 1991/895 as amended and sections 85 and 86 of the Children Act). This is in addition to their duty in respect to children and young people in their care in hospitals or nursing homes in England and Wales as required by section 116 of the Act. Local authorities should take such other steps in relation to the patient while in hospital or nursing home as would be expected to be taken by his or her parent.

39.57 Local authorities are under a duty to:

- promote contact between children and young people who are in need and their families if they live away from home and to help them get back together (paragraphs 10 and 15 of Schedule 2 to the Children Act); and

- arrange for persons (independent visitors) to visit and befriend children and young people looked after by the authority wherever they are if they have not been regularly visited by their parents (paragraph 17 of Schedule 2 to the Act).

39.58 Local authorities should be alerted where the whereabouts of the person with parental responsibility is not known or where that person has not visited the child or young person for a significant period. When alerted to this situation the local authority should consider whether visits should be arranged as under paragraph 39.56.

Under 16s – decisions regarding treatment for mental disorder and deprivation of liberty (or both)

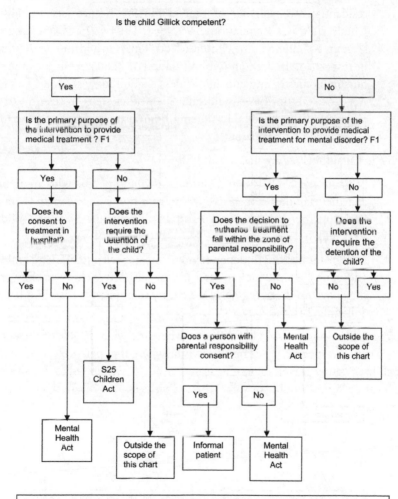

F1 – the treatment may be provided either as part of the assessment under Section 2 or Section 3

16/17s – decisions regarding treatment for mental disorder and/or deprivation of liberty

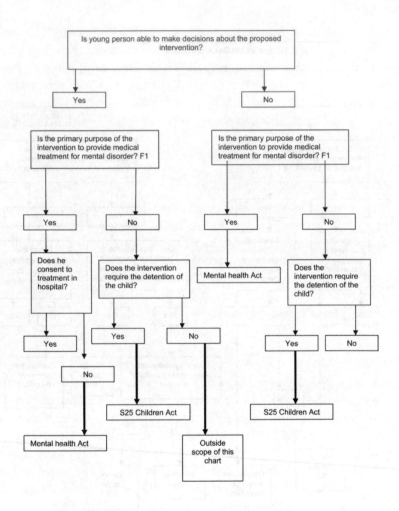

Examples

39.59 The following examples should be read in conjunction with the flow charts.

Example A

A 13 year old child. Assessed as not being Gillick competent. The primary purpose of the intervention is to provide medical treatment for mental disorder. The decision to authorise treatment falls within the zone of parental responsibility as what is proposed is fairly standard, but no person with parental responsibility consents. The child should be admitted to hospital for assessment (section 2) or for treatment (section 3) under the Mental Health Act if they meet the relevant criteria.

Example B

A 14 year old child. Assessed as not being Gillick competent. The primary purpose of the intervention is to provide medical treatment for mental disorder, but she is severely anorexic and this will involve force feeding. This is likely to take it outside the zone of parental responsibility, so even though a person with parental responsibility consents, the child should still be admitted to hospital for assessment (section 2) or for treatment (section 3) under the Mental Health Act if they meet the relevant criteria.

Example C

A 15 year old child. Assessed as being Gillick competent. The primary purpose of the intervention is to provide medical treatment for mental disorder. The child does not consent to treatment in hospital. The child's parents are keen for the child to be admitted to hospital and give their consent. However, it is not considered safe to rely on the parent's consent where a Gillick competent child is refusing. The child should be admitted to hospital for assessment (section 2) or for treatment (section 3) under the Mental Health Act if they meet the relevant criteria.

Example D

A 16 year old. Assessed as being able to make decisions about the proposed intervention. The primary purpose of the intervention is to provide medical treatment for mental disorder. The young person consents to treatment in hospital. The young person should be treated as an informal patient.

Example E

A 17 year old. Assessed as not having the capacity to make decisions about the proposed intervention. The Mental Capacity Act could be used to authorise treatment if the conditions for its use are met, but the primary purpose of the intervention is not to provide medical treatment for mental disorder but to detain the child. Consideration should be given to using section 25 of the Children Act.

Appendix 4

The 2005 Mental Capacity Code of Practice: Chapter 12 – How Does the Act Apply to Children and Young People?

This chapter looks at the few parts of the Act that may affect children under 16 years of age. It also explains the position of young people aged 16 and 17 years and the overlapping laws that affect them.

This chapter does not deal with research. Further guidance will be provided on how the Act applies in relation to research involving those under the age of 18. Within this Code of Practice, 'children' refers to people aged below 16. 'Young people' refers to people aged 16–17. This differs from the Children Act 1989 and the law more generally, where the term 'child' is used to refer to people aged under 18.

In this chapter, as throughout the Code, a person's capacity (or lack of capacity) refers specifically to their capacity to make a particular decision at the time it needs to be made.

Quick summary
CHILDREN UNDER 16

- The Act does not generally apply to people under the age of 16.

- There are two exceptions:

    ○ The Court of Protection can make decisions about a child's property or finances (or appoint a deputy to make these decisions) if the child lacks capacity to make such decisions within section 2(1) of the Act and is likely to still lack capacity to make financial decisions when they reach the age of 18 (section 18(3)).

○ Offences of ill treatment or wilful neglect of a person who lacks capacity within section 2(1) can also apply to victims younger than 16 (section 44).

YOUNG PEOPLE AGED 16–17 YEARS

• Most of the Act applies to young people aged 16–17 years, who may lack capacity within section 2(1) to make specific decisions.

• There are three exceptions:

○ Only people aged 18 and over can make a Lasting Power of Attorney (LPA).

○ Only people aged 18 and over can make an advance decision to refuse medical treatment.

○ The Court of Protection may only make a statutory will for a person aged 18 and over.

CARE OR TREATMENT FOR YOUNG PEOPLE AGED 16–17

• People carrying out acts in connection with the care or treatment of a young person aged 16–17 who lacks capacity to consent within section 2(1) will generally have protection from liability (section 5), as long as the person carrying out the act:

○ has taken reasonable steps to establish that the young person lacks capacity

○ reasonably believes that the young person lacks capacity and that the act is in the young person's best interests, and

○ follows the Act's principles.

• When assessing the young person's best interests (see chapter 5), the person providing care or treatment must consult those involved in the young person's care and anyone interested in their welfare – if it is practical and appropriate to do so. This may include the young person's parents. Care should be taken not to unlawfully breach the young person's right to confidentiality (see chapter 16).

- Nothing in section 5 excludes a person's civil liability for loss or damage, or his criminal liability, resulting from his negligence in carrying out the act.

LEGAL PROCEEDINGS INVOLVING YOUNG PEOPLE AGED 16–17

- Sometimes there will be disagreements about the care, treatment or welfare of a young person aged 16 or 17 who lacks capacity to make relevant decisions. Depending on the circumstances, the case may be heard in the family courts or the Court of Protection.

- The Court of Protection may transfer a case to the family courts, and vice versa.

Does the Act apply to children?

12.1 Section 2(5) of the Act states that, with the exception of section 2(6), as explained below, no powers under the Act may be exercised in relation to a child under 16.

12.2 Care and treatment of children under the age of 16 is generally governed by common law principles. Further information is provided at www.dh.gov.uk/consent (accessed 16.12.07).

Can the Act help with decisions about a child's property or finances?

12.3 Section 2(6) makes an exception for some decisions about a child's property and financial affairs. The Court of Protection can make decisions about property and affairs of those under 16 in cases where the person is likely to still lack capacity to make financial decisions after reaching the age of 18. The court's ruling will still apply when the person reaches the age of 18, which means there will not be a need for further court proceedings once the person reaches the age of 18.

12.4 The Court of Protection can:

- make an order (for example, concerning the investment of an award of compensation for the child), and/or

- appoint a deputy to manage the child's property and affairs and to make ongoing financial decisions on the child's behalf.

In making a decision, the court must follow the Act's principles and decide in the child's best interests as set out in chapter 5 of the Code.

Scenario: Applying the Act to children

Tom was nine when a drunk driver knocked him off his bicycle. He suffered severe head injuries and permanent brain damage. He received a large amount of money in compensation. He is unlikely to recover enough to be able to make financial decisions when he is 18. So the Court of Protection appoints Tom's father as deputy to manage his financial affairs in order to pay for the care Tom will need in the future.

What if somebody mistreats or neglects a child who lacks capacity?

12.5 Section 44 covers the offences of ill treatment or wilful neglect of a person who lacks capacity to make relevant decisions (see chapter 14). This section also applies to children under 16 and young people aged 16 or 17. But it only applies if the child's lack of capacity to make a decision for themselves is caused by an impairment or disturbance that affects how their mind or brain works (see chapter 4). If the lack of capacity is solely the result of the child's youth or immaturity, then the ill treatment or wilful neglect would be dealt with under the separate offences of child cruelty or neglect.

Does the Act apply to young people aged 16–17?

12.6 Most of the Act applies to people aged 16 years and over. There is an overlap with the Children Act 1989. For the Act to apply to a young person, they must lack capacity to make a particular decision (in line with the Act's definition of lack of capacity described in chapter 4). In such situations either this Act or the Children Act 1989 may apply, depending upon the particular circumstances.

However, there may also be situations where neither of these Acts provides an appropriate solution. In such cases, it may be necessary to look to the powers available under the Mental Health Act 1983 or the High Court's inherent powers to deal with cases involving young people.

12.7 There are currently no specific rules for deciding when to use either the Children Act 1989 or the Mental Capacity Act 2005 or when to apply to the High Court. But, the examples below show circumstances where this Act may be the most appropriate (see also paragraphs 12.21–12.23 below).

- In unusual circumstances it might be in a young person's best interests for the Court of Protection to make an order and/or appoint a property and affairs deputy. For example, this might occur when a young person receives financial compensation and the court appoints a parent or a solicitor as a property and affairs deputy.

- It may be appropriate for the Court of Protection to make a welfare decision concerning a young person who lacks capacity to decide for themselves (for example, about where the young person should live) if the court decides that the parents are not acting in the young person's best interests.

- It might be appropriate to refer a case to the Court of Protection where there is disagreement between a person interested in the care and welfare of a young person and the young person's medical team about the young person's best interests or capacity.

Do any parts of the Act not apply to young people aged 16 or 17?

LPAs

12.8 Only people aged 18 or over can make a Lasting Power of Attorney (LPA) (section 9(2)(c)).

Advance decisions to refuse treatment

12.9 Information on decisions to refuse treatment made in advance by young people under the age of 18 will be available at www.dh.gov.uk/consent (accessed 16.12.07).

Making a will

12.10 The law generally does not allow anyone below the age of 18 to make a will. So section 18(2) confirms that the Court of Protection can only make a statutory will on behalf of those aged 18 and over.

What does the Act say about care or treatment of young people aged 16 or 17?

Background information concerning competent young people

12.11 The Family Law Reform Act 1969 presumes that young people have the legal capacity to agree to surgical, medical or dental treatment.[1] This also applies to any associated procedures (for example, investigations, anaesthesia or nursing care).

12.12 It does not apply to some rarer types of procedure (for example, organ donation or other procedures which are not therapeutic for the young person) or research. In those cases, anyone under 18 is presumed to lack legal capacity, subject to the test of 'Gillick competence' (testing whether they are mature and intelligent enough to understand a proposed treatment or procedure).[2]

12.13 Even where a young person is presumed to have legal capacity to consent to treatment, they may not necessarily be able to make the relevant decision. As with adults, decision-makers should assess the young person's capacity to consent to the proposed care or treatment (see chapter 4). If a young person lacks capacity to consent within section 2(1) of the Act because of an impairment of, or a disturbance in the functioning of, the mind or brain then the Mental Capacity Act will apply in the same way as it does to those who are 18 and over. If however they are unable to make the decision for some other reason, for example because they are overwhelmed by the implications of the decision, the Act will not apply to them and the legality of any treatment should be assessed under common law principles.

12.14 If a young person has capacity to agree to treatment, their decision to consent must be respected. Difficult issues can arise if a young person has legal and mental capacity and refuses consent – especially if a person with parental responsibility wishes to give consent on the young person's behalf. The Family Division of the High Court can hear cases where there is disagreement. The

---

1   Family Law Reform Act 1969, section 8(1).
2   In the case of Gillick v West Norfolk and Wisbech Area Health Authority [1986] 1 AC 112 the court found that a child below 16 years of age will be competent to consent to medical treatment if they have sufficient intelligence and understanding to understand what is proposed. This test applies in relation to all people under 18 where there is no presumption of competence in relation to the procedure – for example where the procedure is not one referred to in section 8 of the Family Law Reform Act 1969, e.g. organ donation.

Court of Protection has no power to settle a dispute about a young person who is said to have the mental capacity to make the specific decision.

12.15 It may be unclear whether a young person lacks capacity within section 2(1) of the Act. In those circumstances, it would be prudent for the person providing care or treatment for the young person to seek a declaration from the court.

If the young person lacks capacity to make care or treatment decisions

12.16 Under the common law, a person with parental responsibility for a young person is generally able to consent to the young person receiving care or medical treatment where they lack capacity under section 2(1) of the Act. They should act in the young person's best interests.

12.17 However if a young person lacks the mental capacity to make a specific care or treatment decision within section 2(1) of the Act, healthcare staff providing treatment, or a person providing care to the young person, can carry out treatment or care with protection from liability (section 5) whether or not a person with parental responsibility consents.[3] They must follow the Act's principles and make sure that the actions they carry out are in the young person's best interests. They must make every effort to work out and consider the young person's wishes, feelings, beliefs and values – both past and present – and consider all other factors in the best interests checklist (see chapter 5).

12.18 When assessing a young person's best interests, healthcare staff must take into account the views of anyone involved in caring for the young person and anyone interested in their welfare, where it is practical and appropriate to do so. This may include the young person's parents and others with parental responsibility for the young person. Care should be taken not to unlawfully breach the young person's right to confidentiality (see chapter 16).

12.19 If a young person has said they do not want their parents to be consulted, it may not be appropriate to involve them (for example, where there have been allegations of abuse).

12.20 If there is a disagreement about whether the proposed care or treatment is in the best interests of a young person, or there is disagreement about whether

---

3   Nothing in section 5 excludes a person's civil liability for loss or damage, or his criminal liability, resulting from his negligence in doing the act.

the young person lacks capacity and there is no other way of resolving the matter, it would be prudent for those in disagreement to seek a declaration or other order from the appropriate court (see paragraphs 12.23–12.25 below).

Scenario: Working out a young person's best interests

Mary is 16 and has Down's syndrome. Her mother wants Mary to have dental treatment that will improve her appearance but is not otherwise necessary.

To be protected under section 5 of the Act, the dentist must consider whether Mary has capacity to agree to the treatment and what would be in her best interests. He decides that she is unable to understand what is involved or the possible consequences of the proposed treatment and so lacks capacity to make the decision.

But Mary seems to want the treatment, so he takes her views into account in deciding whether the treatment is in her best interests. He also consults with both her parents and with her teacher and GP to see if there are other relevant factors to take into account.

He decides that the treatment is likely to improve Mary's confidence and self-esteem and is in her best interests.

12.21 There may be particular difficulties where young people with mental health problems require in-patient psychiatric treatment, and are treated informally rather than detained under the Mental Health Act 1983. The Mental Capacity Act and its principles apply to decisions related to the care and treatment of young people who lack mental capacity to consent, including treatment for mental disorder. As with any other form of treatment, somebody assessing a young person's best interests should consult anyone involved in caring for the young person or anyone interested in their welfare, as far as is practical and appropriate. This may include the young person's parents or those with parental responsibility for the young person.

But the Act does not allow any actions that result in a young person being deprived of their liberty (see chapter 6). In such circumstances, detention under the Mental Health Act 1983 and the safeguards provided under that Act might be appropriate (see also chapter 13).

12.22 People may disagree about a young person's capacity to make the specific decision or about their best interests, or it may not be clear whether they lack capacity within section 2(1) or for some other reason. In this situation, legal proceedings may be necessary if there is no other way of settling the disagreement (see chapters 8 and 15). If those involved in caring for the young person or who are interested in the young person's welfare do not agree with the proposed treatment, it may be necessary for an interested party to make an application to the appropriate court.

What powers do the courts have in cases involving young people?

12.23 A case involving a young person who lacks mental capacity to make a specific decision could be heard in the family courts (probably in the Family Division of the High Court) or in the Court of Protection.

12.24 If a case might require an ongoing order (because the young person is likely to still lack capacity when they are 18), it may be more appropriate for the Court of Protection to hear the case. For one-off cases not involving property or finances, the Family Division may be more appropriate.

12.25 So that the appropriate court hears a case, the Court of Protection can transfer cases to the family courts, and vice versa (section 21).

Scenario: Hearing cases in the appropriate court

Shola is 17. She has serious learning disabilities and lacks the capacity to decide where she should live. Her parents are involved in a bitter divorce. They cannot agree on several issues concerning Shola's care – including where she should live. Her mother wants to continue to look after Shola at home. But her father wants Shola to move into a care home.

   In this case, it may be more appropriate for the Court of Protection to deal with the case. This is because an order made in the Court of Protection could continue into Shola's adulthood. However an order made by the family court under the Children Act 1989 would end on Shola's eighteenth birthday.

Subject Index

Index of Legislation and Guidance

244 Children with Mental Disorder and the Law

Office of the Children's
Commissioner *Pushed into the
Shadows: Young People's
Experience of Adult Mental
Health Facilities* 22

Police and Criminal Evidence Act
1984 92
Powers of Criminal Court
(Sentencing) Act 2000 100,
101

R (A) v. Partnerships in Care Ltd
[2002] 24
*R (Axon) v. The Secretary of State for
Health and the Family Planning
Association* [2006] 184, 185
R (B) v. Dr SS and others (2005) 26
*R (H) v. London North and East Region
Mental Health Review Tribunal
(Secretary of State Intervening)*
[2001] 23
R (JB) v. Haddock and others (2006)
26
R (N) v. Dr M and others (2002) 26
*R (on the application of H) v. Secretary
of State for Health* [2005] 88,
89
*R (on the application of DR) v. Mersey
Health Care NHS Trust* [2002]
85
R (on the application of H) v. MHRT
[2000] 64, 104
R (PS) v. RMO and SOAD (2003) 26
*R (Wilkinson) v. (1) Broadmoor
Hospital Authority, (2) the Mental
Health Act Commission, (3)
Secretary of State for Health*
(2002) 26
*R v. Ashworth Hospital Authority (now
Mersey Care NHS Trust) ex parte
Munjaz* [2005] 60
*R v. Cambridge Health Authority ex
parte B* [1995] 121
*R v. Collins and Ashworth Hospital
Authority ex parte Brady* [2000]
74
R v. Gardner ex parte L [1986] 84
R v. Hallstrom ex parte W [1986] 84
*R v. Kirklees Metropolitan Borough
Council (MBC) ex parte C
(QBD)* [1992] 69
*R v. London Borough of Barnet ex parte
B* [1994] 121

*R v. Manchester City Council ex parte
Stennett* [2002] 127
*R v. MHRT for the South Thames
Region ex parte Smith* [1999] 73
*R v. North West London Mental Health
NHS Trust ex parte Stewart*
[1997] 101
*R v. Northampton Juvenile Court ex
parte London Borough of
Hammersmith and Fulham* [1985]
52
R v. Wilson ex parte Williamson
[1996] 81
*Re B (Care: Interference with Family
Life)* [2003] 32
*Re C (Adult: Refusal of Medical
Treatment)* [1994] 74
Re C (Detention: Medical Treatment)
[1997] 53
*Re F (Mental Health Act:
Guardianship)* [2000] 72, 96,
115
*Re G (Interim Care Order: Residential
Assessment)* [2004] 45
Re G (Secure Accommodation) [2000]
56
*Re H and R (Child Sexual Abuse:
Standard of Proof)* [1996] 43
*Re K (Secure Accommodation Order:
Right to Liberty)* [2001] 12, 29,
30, 58, 71
*Re K, W and H (Minors) (Medical
Treatment)* [1993] 192, 193,
196, 197
*Re M (A Minor) (Care Order:
Threshold Conditions)* [1994] 43
Re M (Medical Treatment) [1999]
186
Re M (Secure Accommodation Order)
[1995] 56
Re MB (Medical Treatment) [1997]
109
Re R (A Minor) (Blood Transfusion)
[1993] 41
*Re R (A Minor) (Wardship: Medical
Treatment)* [1991] 114, 188,
190–1, 194, 195
Re S and W (Care Proceedings) [2007]
46
*Re SA (Vulnerable Adult with Capacity:
Marriage)* [2006] 116
Re W (A Minor) (Medical Treatment)
[1992] 192, 194–5

*Re W (A Minor) (Secure
Accommodation Order)* [1993]
54
Report of the Committee on the
Age of Majority (Cmnd 3342)
(1967) 189
Riverside Health NHS Trust v. Fox
[1994] 74

Secretary of State for Health and
the Home Secretary (2000)
*Reforming the Mental Health Act
Part 1: The New Legal Framework*
(Cm 5016–1) 200
*South Glamorgan County Council v. W
and B)* [1993] 45

T and V v. United Kingdom [2000]
31
*Tameside and Glossop Acute Services
Trust v. CH* [1996] 75
*The Queen on the application of S v.
Plymouth City Council (C as
interested party)* [2002] 180
*Too Serious a Thing: The Review of
Safeguards for Young People
Treated and Cared for by the NHS
in Wales* (2002) 128
Tyrer v. United Kingdom (1978) 25

W v. L [1973] 67
W v. United Kingdom [1987] 31
Wall J 195
Winterwerp v. Netherlands (1979) 87

*YL v. Birmingham City Council and
others* [2007] 24

Author Index